Opium

Francis Moraes, Ph.D.
Debra Moraes, M.A.

RONIN
Berkeley, CA

Opium

ISBN: 0-914171-83-6

Copyright © 2003 by Francis Moraes & Debra Moraes

From *The Little Book* Series

Published by

RONIN Publishing, Inc.

PO Box 22900

Oakland, CA 94609

www.roninpub.com

Credits:

Editor:	**Beverly A. Potter,** www.docpotter.com
Copy Editor:	**Amy Demmon**
Cover:	**Judy July,** Generic Typograpy
Illustrations:	**Alexander King,** from *Black Opium,* Claude Farrere, And/Or Press, 1974
Fonts:	Avant Garde
	Goudy Old Style
	Harrington
	Park Avenue

Distributed to the trade by **Publishers Group West**

Printed in the United States of America by Arvato/Bertelsmann

Library of Congress Card Number – 2003107666

Printing Number 1

Table of Contents

1
Myths

OPIUM! No other drug conjures such romantic images of distant times and places. Southeast Asian farmers surrounded by acres of crimson flowers. Nodding thrill-seekers inhaling white vapors in a Chinatown opium den. The writer sipping laudanum as he translates his last three-hour opium dream into one of the greatest poems in the English language. There is no end to the images.

Dreaded Agent

OPIUM IS NOT A DRUG; IT'S A MYTH. Laws have made opium all but disappear in favor of the far more potent opium-derivative, heroin. But more important, there is something self-mythologizing about opium. It reeks of otherworldliness—maybe heaven, maybe hell, maybe both.

On hearing opium mentioned for the first time as a potential cure for his rheumatic pains, Thomas De Quincey, the esteemed 19th Century journalist and essayist, reacted much the same as we do today: "Opium! [D]read agent of unimaginable pleasure and pain! I had heard of it as I heard of manna or of ambrosia, but no further."

Changing the World

THERE ARE MANY REASONS to think of opium with a mixture of fear and fascination. It changes our sense of reality; we see the world differently. For the person under the influence, the world has changed. One dose of opium can turn an uptight corporate CEO into a Taoist philosopher, at least as long as the opium effects last.

Noodles, the gangster in the movie *Once Upon a Time in America*, physically escaped into Chinatown opium dens in order to mentally escape the violent world in which he was trapped. This romantic image of a sensitive gangster beneath the tough exterior illustrates how opium has the power to change one's view of the world.

Destroyer of Grief

CALLED "DESTROYER OF GRIEF" and "God's own medicine" since antiquity, opium has been used to change the way people look at their lives. Throughout the 19th Century, opium was used in countless patent medicines claiming to cure "nervous ailments" such as depression and anxiety. Opium could be counted on to change a person's outlook on life for the better. But if that were ■■■■■■ the whole story of opium, we wouldn't

Addiction is a trap.

need to talk about it—we'd just enjoy it.

In the United States in 1900, opium could be bought by anyone, in any quantity as often as one wished. Yet less than 1% of the population used it habitually, which is far less than today. This low number seems odd. Certainly the "destroyer of grief" would be found useful to a lot more people than that! It was, but the vast majority of people used opium only when there was a medical reason to do so.

Comparing United States opium users in 1900 to opium users today is difficult. In 1900, not all people used opium directly. They may have used morphine, codeine, and heroin. Today, only a few use opium. Instead, they use one or more of the dizzying number of opium derived or inspired drugs. In addition, we cannot compare the total number of opium users in 1900 to the current users of illegal opium drugs. Many, if not most, of the opium users in 1900 were using the drug for purposes that would be considered therapeutic and not abusive. If these people were alive today, they would be getting an opium-like drug from a doctor, and so would not be counted as an illegal drug user in government statistics.

Price of Paradise

THERE ARE MANY REASONS the majority of people limited their opium use, without being compelled to do so by law. People kept a safe distance from "God's own medicine" to avoid the hell of addiction. The hell of a heroin addict kicking cold turkey hasn't changed for hundreds of years. An opium addict without "medicine" screams in pain and is drenched in sweat, while suffering chills and vomiting. This torturous experience goes on for a week or more.

More than alone, however, people sensed that addiction was a trap—a treadmill leading nowhere. Life becomes more and more dedicated to tending to the addiction, until seeking opium is the only thing left. This is why addiction is so often analogized as slavery.

It is a myth, however, that use goes up without limit. Users eventually stabilize their daily dosage, just like with cigarettes, coffee, and alcohol. But just as with cigarettes, coffee, and alcohol, opium addiction is a burden.

Opium becomes myth for those who have used it as well as those who have not. It is heaven and hell all rolled into one. Opium is a Calvinist's idea of earthly sin punishment. It is karma applied to happiness. It is Dad's old admonition: "You can't have your cake and eat it, too!" Destroyer of grief? Ha! It is the creator of grief!

Rooted in Truth

THE MYTHOLOGY OF OPIUM IS ROOTED IN TRUTH. The myth provides important and correct information about this romanticized drug. Opium is the most important natural medicinal substance available to humankind. To this very day, it is responsible for the most effective painkillers. Much of what we know about how the brain works comes from the study of opium. It has been used for millennia in religious ceremonies. Perhaps most telling of all is that millions of people spend huge amounts of money on the black market, risking jail and even death to use opium and its derivatives. Any substance this important deserves to be judged on facts, not myths. Yet, the more facts we discover about opium, the more we seem to judge it on myth.

The Journey Begins

THE REAL STORY OF OPIUM IS COMPLEX, as are all real stories. As opium took a circuitous journey from culture to culture around the world, so too shall we take a circuitous journey to understand this fascinating substance. We will explore botany, chemistry, biology, political science, agriculture, linguistics, sociology, law, and many other subjects. In learning the facts about opium, we will also better understand the mythology.

2
What is Opium?

OPIUM IS A COMPLEX DRUG that cannot be trivialized with a short condensation of its effects. This is to be expected. Why would so many people spend their whole lives dedicated to it—as users, researchers, writers, and even haters—if it were any other way? Surely they would become bored with a simpler substance. How many times can one ride the same rollercoaster before it becomes, well, predictable and boring?

Not One Drug

MOST DRUGS ARE SINGLE CHEMICAL COMPOUNDS that can be defined with a chemical formula. For example, methamphetamine is $C_{10}H_{15}N$ and LSD is $C_{20}H_{25}N_3O$. When a person takes a pill, it is usually one or two drugs. Aspirin, for example, is comprised of only one drug. Vicodin®—5 mg of hydrocodone and 500 mg of acetaminophen—isan example of two drugs combined to create one medicine.

This is not so in the case of opium. Opium isn't a single drug or even a set collection of drugs. The constituents of every sample of opium are different, which makes it hard to come to a holistic understanding of opium. Simple legal or scientific definitions are also difficult. Definitions provide insights, however, so we will look at some.

Definitions

DEFINITIONS OF OPIUM generally fall into one of three categories: creation, content, and effect. In the creation-based definition, we describe how opium is created. When these steps are followed the result is a substance that we define as opium. In the content-based definition, we say that the stuff we've been calling opium contains certain chemicals in certain concentrations. When a substance has more or less the same composition, we define it as "opium." In the third definition, we say that any drug that makes a person feel a particular way is opium. These definitions are helpful in understanding what opium is, even if the ultimate definition is, and will always be, murkier than we might like.

Creation Definition

OPIUM CAN BE DEFINED by how it is created. The ripe seedpods of opium poppies are cut in two. Latex from the poppies seep out of these incisions and dry on the outside of the pods. This dry substance is defined as opium.

The creation definition is deceptive in a couple of ways. Substances that are very much like what we think of as opium can be produced from poppies other than the Opium variety, such as the Common Poppy, or *Papaver rhoeas*. Secondly, an opium-like substance can be extracted by crushing and purifying poppies. Although not opium, this poppy straw does contain all the chemicals found in opium.

> Opium is heaven and hell all rolled into one.

Still, the creation definition is commonly used and provides useful generalities. First, opium comes from certain kinds of poppies. Second, opium is concentrated in the seedpod of the plant. Third, it directly comes from the poppy, much as cactus juice comes from a cactus. Little has to be done to create opium.

Content Definition

OPIUM CAN BE DEFINED by its content. This is because opium is made up of roughly fifty drug-like compounds known as alkaloids. The problem with this definition is that the proportions of the alkaloids found in opium vary from batch to batch. For example, morphine, which is the alkaloid in highest abundance, can range from less than 10% to as high as 20%. That is a big margin of error.

> *Opium can be defined by its content.*

On the other hand, the content definition does have its uses. It tells us what will be found in any opium sample. What's more, the proportions are fairly well determined, especially for commercially produced opium.

Effects Definition

THE DEFINITION BASED ON OPIUM'S EFFECT is the most problematic. But a thousand years ago, it was almost perfect. The reason is that at that time, science had not plunged inside opium to unravel its secrets. The only drug that affected the body like opium was opium. But since then, many chemicals have been discovered to have effects similar to those of opium.

Still, the effects definition is useful and more to the point of the drug than the other definitions. Opium makes a person feel safe and relaxed—happy, in a very detached way. It places him in a dreamy state that is much like sleep. In the simplest but most profound sense, opium makes anyone who uses it feel contented.

Working Definition

WE WILL REFINE THE DEFINITION OF OPIUM as we move along. For the time, however, it is helpful to have a working definition. We will use the following brief definition of this complicated drug.

Working Definition:

Opium is a complex drug composed of many
distinct chemicals, each with different effects.
The overall effect of opium is to make one feel at
ease, relaxed, contented. It is the source of many
important medicines—especially pain medicines.

3

Opium Effects

OPIUM IS A COMBINATION of many different drugs. Consequently, its effects are more complex than those of a pure substance—such as methamphetamine. The majority of opium's effects comes from morphine, its primary constituent. However, opium is not simply unrefined morphine. The effects of opium are far more complex. You might think of it as the difference between a charcoal sketch and an oil painting of the same object. The sketch is detailed and beautiful, but the painting has more depth and nuance.

It is confusing that opium is a drug but also *contains* drugs. It is more accurate to say that opium is a substance that contains a number of drugs. Doing so is cumbersome and so we refer to opium as simply "a drug." There should be no problem with this, however. Modern medicine has many "drugs" that are really combinations of drugs. "Drugs" for cold sufferers are a combination of drugs. Excedrin®—the headache "drug"—is a combination of the three drugs acetaminophen, aspirin, and caffeine. The prescription "drug" Vicodin® combines acetaminophen and hydrocodone.

> Opium is a drug but also contains drugs.

Comparison

OPIUM AND THE DRUGS DERIVED from it make up a

▬▬▬▬   distinct class of drugs known as the opio-

Opium   ids. Whereas most drugs have similarities

is only   to other drugs, this is not really true of

                    opium. Cocaine, for example, is similar in

similar   many ways to methamphetamine.

to itself.   Marijuana's effects are similar to LSD.

Opium is only similar to itself. The only drugs that feel like opium are the alkaloids actually found in opium, such as morphine, and alkaloids derived from them, such as Dilaudid®.

Five Drug Categories

IN 1924, DURING PROHIBITION, a German chemist name Louis Lewin published a hugely influential book titled *Phantastica: Narcotic and Stimulating Drugs.* For the first time in the study of drugs, Lewin subdivided them by their effects. He described five categories, which are as applicable today as they were in the early 20th Century, despite the invention of new substances like crack cocaine and "designer drugs." The categories are euphoriants, excitants, hypnotics, inebriants, and phantasticants.

Drug Categories

Category	Description	Example
Euphoriants	Contentmen	Morphine
Excitants	Alertness	Methamphetamine
Hypnotics	Sleep	Valium®
Inebriants	Intoxication	Ethanol
Phantasticants	Hallucination	THC

Euphoriants are drugs that lower the intensity of unpleasant emotions. Excitants, as the name implies, stimulate mental processing. Hypnotics produce sleep. Inebriants produce distorted perception, thinking, and feeling. Phantasticants produce hallucinations.

Crossovers

MANY DRUGS CROSS BOUNDARIES. Alcohol, for example, can be said to exist partly in all the categories. It produces intoxication and is thus an inebriant, of course. But alcohol also produces sleep and euphoria. At extremely high doses, it can produce hallucinations, while at very small doses, it can increase alertness—like an excitant does.

Opium, on the other hand, has little crossover into the other categories. It does not excite, although its analgesic ability does enable people to do physical activities that would otherwise be too difficult or painful. Opium does cause nodding, but it is not actual sleep; opium interferes with sleep. Opium does not distort the cognitive abilities, thinking is just slowed. Finally, "opium dreams," which are sometimes erroneously referred to as hallucinations, are clearly not.

THE SHOCKING ECSTASY OF THE FORBIDD

G-120

35¢

BLACK OPIUM

Claude Farrère

COMPLETE AND UNABRIDGED

Opium has been a tantilizing subject for writers for hundreds of years.

Contentment

THE FEELING OF CONTENTMENT is the essential aspect of the opium "high." It is a common misconception that drugs provide some form of contentment—it represents much of the drug's appeal. Actually, feelings of contentment are characteristic only of the opioids. Cocaine users know very well the feeling of continual discontentment. They never quite get high enough and never achieve the feeling they sense that the drug could provide.

The opium high is subtle. It is similar to what one experiences when happy. The first written reference about opium discusses its usefulness as a cure for diarrhea. Additionally, slowed respiration and not euphoria was the first effect noticed of the drug heroin—the powerful opium derivative.

While the effect of opium on mental state is subtle, it is also profound. When using opium, one is contented to do whatever he is doing, regardless of how painful or boring the activity may be. Chinese railroad workers in 19th Century United States were noted for working productively without complaint for long hours because of their use of opium. Opium makes people happy with any situation they happen to be in. Here's how one person we interviewed puts it:

We had spent the previous night smoking opium. We slept in a grass hut with a dirt floor, on a bed of bamboo raised two feet from the floor. I remember feeling such ecstasy that I understood for the first time how addicts could live in rooms with dirty floors, peeling paint, and a naked light bulb hanging from the ceiling—all without a care.

Nodding

MANY ASSOCIATE OPIUM WITH SLEEP. In *The Wizard of Oz*, Dorothy wandered off the road of yellow bricks into a field of scarlet poppies, nearly falling asleep. She was saved by her friends who hurried her back onto the road.

> *They carried the sleeping girl to a pretty spot beside the river, far enough from the poppy field to prevent her breathing any more of the poison of the flowers, and here they laid her gently on the soft grass and waited for the fresh breeze to waken her.*

In moderate doses, opium does not produce sleep. What it does produce is a phenomenon commonly called *nodding*, which is a semi-consciousness state characterized by "opium dreams," which are a cross between sleeping dreams and daydreams. The dreamer can often control what happens in these dreams. This ability is combined with a richness of imagery from the unhindered right brain. A long history of artists—such as Edgar Allan Poe—used opium as a creative tool.

Sex

OPIUM IS OFTEN USED AS AN APHRODISIAC. Like other aphrodisiacs, opium does not to turn one into a nymphomaniac; rather it encourages latent desires and loosens inhibitions.

Under the influence of opium, one becomes sensitive to touch in a positive way. Being rubbed, scratched, and caressed feels marvelous. Lone opium indulgers often notice that their bodies itch—especially their noses—and take great pleasure scratching. Lovers can spend hours touching, massaging, and even scratching one another. One woman we interviewed described her first opium experience in just this way:

> *He looked at me, knowing from where I came from. Leading me to bed, he disrobed me. He could have done anything he wanted, but he knew what would give me greatest pleasur—not sex, but sensuality. He began by lightly scratching my body. First my back, then my legs, eventually even I cannot recall—so lost in ecstasy was I.*

When using opium, one can become more in touch with the primal self. Dell Pendell describes the rare orgasm while under the influence of opium. When the climax is at last achieved, it seems to split the spine. In an instant one knows what lizards feel when they mate, and why they clamber onto a sun-warmed rock in the morning.

Negative Effects

OPIUM'S EFFECTS ARE NOT ALL PLEASANT, however. It can cause severe nausea and vomiting, especially when one moves around a great deal. Many people avoid this discomfort by remaining quiet and still. For others, nothing can lessen the discomfort, which can be overwhelming.

Opium's effects are not all pleasant.

There are drugs that effectively relieve the nausea associated with opium, but they are either illegal or controlled. Some people combine opium with marijuana, which is an effective anti-nausea drug. Opium and marijuana rolled into a cigarette is sometimes called an OJ, which is short for "Opium Joint." Opium can also cause great anxiety, particularly in addicts.

Therapeutic Effects

OPIUM HAS A NUMBER OF EFFECTS on the human body, which are neither positive nor negative. Opium relieves pain, decreases activity in the intestines, and reduces respiration. These effects have made it an enormously popular therapeutic drug throughout history.

Analgesia

ALONG WITH ITS DERIVATIVES, opium is a powerful analgesic. Analgesics are pain relievers that don't rely upon producing sleep for their effectiveness. Pain is managed in two ways by opium. First, the pain stimulus received by the brain is deadened. Second, the pain felt is perceived as less annoying. One can still feel the pain, but it isn't such a big deal.

Constipation

OPIUM CAUSES CONSTIPATION by sedating the large and small intestines. As a result, it is an excellent cure for diarrhea. In the ancient world, dysentery was common because of a lack of proper sanitation. Dysentery is also a problem today where proper sanitation is absent. Outbreaks cause chronic diarrhea lasting up to six weeks. Diarrhea is considered a minor ailment in prosperous nations, but it can kill by dehydrating the sufferer, especially when he is already weakened from other problems. Opium is a lifesaver to such people. As mentioned before, the first written reference to opium described its usefulness as a cure for diarrhea.

Slowed Breathing

IN THE 1850s, ONE-FIFTH OF ALL DEATHS IN EUROPE and the United States were due to tuberculosis. As a result, there was great interest in drugs that helped those with TB. This eventually led to the development of heroin as a commercial product. Opium doesn't cure tuberculosis. However, those suffering from the disease cough less, because opium reduces respiration levels. This means less pain for the infected, and lower infection rates for the uninfected.

Slowing respiration is also responsible for the most feared aspect of the drug: its ability to kill. Taken in high enough doses, opium can stop breathing altogether. When this happens, it is called a fatal overdose. Although this is more associated with drugs that are injected, one may experience a fatal overdose of opium when eating or smoking.

If people die accidentally, we might wonder if opium could be used as a poison to kill someone. There are some such stories from the Greeks. It is said that Dionysius killed his father with an opium overdose in 367 BC. As we shall see, however, opium is not very toxic. It is rare for someone to die from a fatal opium overdose. As a result, opium is a poor choice for the murderous poisoner. Its effectiveness as a poison, however, would be greatly enhanced if it were combined with other drugs.

In general, it is safer to drink a drug than to smoke it. In the case of opium, however, smoking is less likely to result in a fatal overdose. Smoking is the fastest way to get a drug to the brain. At the same time, it can only deliver a small amount per dose. The opium smoker simply falls asleep when getting too high, and is unable to smoke anymore. In contrast, one can drink almost unlimited amounts of opium before feeling the effect. A fatal overdose may thus result. This is an over-simplification, however.

Why People Like Opium

MANY STUDIES HAVE FOUND that people find the overall effect of opium unpleasant. This seems strange on the face of it. Why is it said then to cause euphoria? Why are there so many opium addicts? The answer is that it is not so much that opium is unpleasant, but that form some people the negative affects of opium overshadow the positive effects.

The nausea caused by opium can be extreme and long lasting. Well over half of all people using opium experience a good deal of nausea, even after considerable experience with its use. The feelings of euphoria and contentment brought on by opium are subtle, whereas the effects of nausea are quite strong. More experienced people don't mind the negative effects of the drug because they learn to "tune into" what they like and "tune out" what they don't. In the movie

Drugstore Cowboy, Rick tells his girlfriend, "Nadine, just go take your half a blue, shoot it, and go puke a while." In other words, Rick is saying, "Go experience something bad because along with it, you will be experiencing something even better."

Opium's Power

OPIUM HAS IMPORTANT, even life-saving, medical uses. But much of its therapeutic power stems from its ability to improve one's mood. Happy people are better able to manage pain. The downside is that people sometimes overuse substances that make them happy. Opium's healing power is the flip-side of its addicting power. Like all powerful things, opium must be respected.

4
Opium Dreams

MUCH OF THE MYSTIQUE that surrounds opium comes from the phenomenon of "opium dreams." Some writers have likened opium dreams to the hallucinations experienced when taking LSD, peyote, and similar drugs. Other writers go so far as to say opium dreams are hallucinations. Although this is a ridiculous contention, there is no doubt that opium is a highly visual drug.

Non-Ordinary Dreams

OPIUM DREAMS ARE SIMILAR TO ORDINARY DREAMS in that they tap into the subconscious and render visual stories for the mind. Like regular dreams, opium dreams are very personal and individual. But that is where the similarity ends. As we discuss opium dreams, keep in mind that we are making generalizations. Everything we say can be contradicted by the direct experience of opium users. These generalities do not constrain the dreams people actually have when using opium.

Opium dreams are distinct from regular dreams in a number of ways. First, opium dreams are usually "lucid." That is, the dreamer is aware of dreaming and can control the flow. Second, opium dreams are far richer

in content than are nighttime dreams. Third, the source
of the dream content is often elusive. And finally, while
regular dreams can be chaotic with one image detached
from another, images normally flow smoothly throughout
opium dreams. When someone describes a sleeping
dream, it contains a lot of phrases like, "Suddenly, I
found myself...." This is an indication of the chaotic
flow of nighttime dreams. It is as though the mind got
bored with the story it was telling and started a new
one. This is one of the reasons dreams fascinate us so.
Opium dreams have twists and turns too, of course, but
there is usually a connective "narrative" from one part
to another.

Lucid Dreams

OPIUM DREAMS are much like what are commonly called
"lucid dreams," dreams in which the dreamer is conscious and able to control the course of the dream.
One might even call them fantasies. This idea is explicit
in the title of one of the poems of Maria White
Lowell.

An Opium Fantasy

Soft hangs the opiate in the brain,
And lulling soothes the edge of pain,
Till harshest sound, far off or near,
Sings floating in its mellow sphere.
What wakes me from my heavy dream?
Or am I still asleep?
Those long and soft vibrations seem
A slumberous charm to keep.

Lowell probably took opium, or perhaps morphine, for tuberculosis. She was the wife of James Russell Lowell, the popular poet and political activist of the 19ᵗʰ Century. Maria is credited for encouraging his literary and political work. She is not well known, however, having died tragically at age 32.

Opium dreams come from deep within the subconscious.

The extent to which a person on opium has control of a dream is probably dose-dependent. For example, heroin is an opium derivative with similar effects, but there are few references made to "heroin dreams." This is likely due to the simplicity and purity of the heroin high as compared to the opium high. Heroin does not produce as much in terms of dream stimuli. But it is probably also due to heroin's much greater potency. Heroin will cause you to dream, but you will be too high to remember, much less control the dream.

Detachment

BECAUSE OF THE WAY THAT OPIUM ACTS on the pleasure centers of the brain, one would think that opium "nightmares" would be rare and generally, this is so. Great pleasure is usually associated with opium dreams. But opium dreams, which deeply probe the right brain, can conjure up dark images. How disturbing such dreams are depends on how much control the dreamer has of the events.

People on opium are usually detached from the dream, as if watching a movie. The most inspired opium dreams are likely to come from large opium doses, however. Under such circumstances, one is likely to have little conscious control of the dream. This can create opium nightmares.

Mary Robinson describes just such a nightmare in her poem *The Maniac*. It has been called the first "opium poem." Although probably an over-statement, it certainly was one of the first in Victorian England. It influenced writers such as Samuel Taylor Coleridge and Thomas de Quincey.

Another unusual aspect of Robinson's dream is that its source is readily found in her daily life, making it different from those of de Quincey and others. The day she had the dream, she had seen what she called "a maniac" on the street.

After taking a large dose of opium, she had the dream. Upon waking, she dictated the 120-line poem to her daughter. The next day, however, Robinson had memory of neither the dream nor of dictating the poem. Note that although the poem is a nightmare, the author speaks with power—indicating a self-control she probably would not have had in an actual encounter.

The Maniac

Fix not thy steadfast gaze on me,
Shrunk atom of mortality!
Nor freeze my blood with thy
    distracted groan;
Ah! quickly turn those eyes away,
They fill my soul with dire dismay,
For dead and dark they seem, and
    almost chill'd to stone!

Others have experienced a similar sense of self-control exerted despite frightening conditions in an opium nightmare. One person we interviewed talked of floating in a dark place populated by other "beings" who were even darker than the space. These beings were all grabbing at him as he moved quickly to avoid their attacks. Eventually, one of the beings did get hold of his leg. As he came back to consciousness, he was fighting with the being in an attempt to break free.

Rich Imagery

OPIUM DREAMS ARE KNOWN for their rich imagery. Perhaps because of their association with distant places, the content of opium dreams is often exotic. This is certainly true of the opium dream experienced by Samuel Taylor Coleridge in 1797. It is no exaggeration to say that it is the most famous opium dream that ever occurred, depicted in his classic poem *Kubla Khan*.

Kubla Khan

In Xanadu did Kubla Khan
A stately pleasure-dome decree:
Where Alph, the sacred river, ran
Through caverns measureless to man
Down to a sunless sea.
So twice five miles of fertile ground
With walls and towers were girdled round:
And here were gardens bright with sinuous rills
Where blossomed many an incense-bearing tree;
And here were forests ancient as the hills,
Enfolding sunny spots of greenery.
But oh! that deep romantic chasm which slanted
Down the green hill athwart a cedarn cover!
A savage place! as holy and enchanted
As e'er beneath a waning moon was haunted
By woman wailing for her demon-lover!
And from this chasm, with ceaseless
     turmoil seething,
    As if this earth in fast thick pants were
    breathing,
    A mighty fountain momently was
    forced;
   Amid whose swift half-intermitted
burst
Huge fragments vaulted like rebounding hail,
Or chaffy grain beneath the thresher's flail:
And 'mid these dancing rocks at once and ever
It flung up momently the sacred river.
Five miles meandering with a mazy motion
Through wood and dale the sacred river ran,

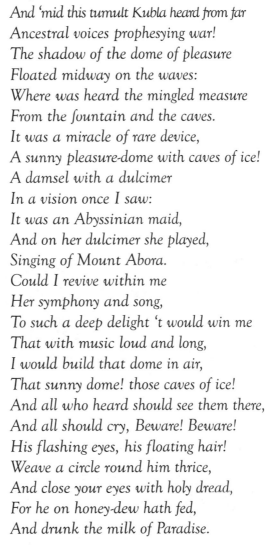

Then reached the
  caverns measure-
  less to man,
And sank in tun
  lifeless ocean:
And 'mid this tumult Kubla heard from far
Ancestral voices prophesying war!
The shadow of the dome of pleasure
Floated midway on the waves:
Where was heard the mingled measure
From the fountain and the caves.
It was a miracle of rare device,
A sunny pleasure-dome with caves of ice!
A damsel with a dulcimer
In a vision once I saw:
It was an Abyssinian maid,
And on her dulcimer she played,
Singing of Mount Abora.
Could I revive within me
Her symphony and song,
To such a deep delight 't would win me
That with music loud and long,
I would build that dome in air,
That sunny dome! those caves of ice!
And all who heard should see them there,
And all should cry, Beware! Beware!
His flashing eyes, his floating hair!
Weave a circle round him thrice,
And close your eyes with holy dread,
For he on honey-dew hath fed,
And drunk the milk of Paradise.

—Samuel Taylor Coleridge

Exactly what Coleridge experienced is unclear. The only thing that is clear is also the only thing that is quantifiable: the amount of opium he took. Coleridge started his experience by drinking two grains—about 130 mg—of opium, which is a fairly large dose.

From then on, his accounts of his opium experience differ and often contradict. By one account, he said he experienced a "profound sleep," and by another "a sort of reverie," or daydream. This may be a simple matter of interpretation, however. Coleridge points out that by "sleep" he means he was inured to external stimuli, implying that while his physical body was resting his mind was awake.

The dream then unfolded for him. To Coleridge it came as if from outside—like a gift from God. Now it is generally agreed that the dream and the resulting poem were the products of his own exceptionally creative mind. Regardless, it was Coleridge who translated the images of the dream into poetic form. It is remarkable to think that a dream lasting three hours—by Coleridge's own account—resulted in just 54 lines of poetry. But these lines are among the most vivid and striking in the whole history of poetry.

"Opium dreams" are due primarily to the morphine contained in opium.

Source Material

OPIUM DREAMS ARE NOT SIMPLY A HODGEPODGE of images from the dreamer's waking hours, like these of ordinary dreams. In many cases, the opium dreamer has no idea where the images came from. It seems that the dreams come from deep within the subconscious or perhaps more creativity is applied to the usual dream stimuli.

Thomas de Quincey reflected on this aspect of opium dreams in his memoirs, *Confessions of an English Opium Eater.* He says that the minutest incidents from his childhood would show up in his opium dreams. During his waking hours, however, he had no recollection of them at all. "But placed as they were before me, in dreams like intuitions, and clothed in all their evanescent circumstances and accompanying feelings, I [recognized] them instantaneously."

Smooth Imagery

OPIUM DREAMS ARE MOST OFTEN DESCRIBED as being "smooth," images flowing from one to another rather than changing abruptly. As a result of this, they tend to be deliberately paced. Opium enthusiasts tend to move slowly, like their dreams. This may be a function of the state of their minds because people on opium are generally happy in any environment. This happy state probably applies to their dreams as well.

A good example of the smoothly flowing imagery of opium dreams is found in a short story by Santa Louise Anderson, in which she rises from her lounge to explore the entire planet. The story begins with her floating up and out of her house.

An Opium Dream

I arose slowly from the lounge, up, up, up, with the light, easy motions of a swimmer. The roof offered no resistance. I passed through it out into the moonlight. A eucalyptus tree was in bloom by the front gate, and I paused on my upward way to look at the blossoms, circling round and round the tree as I did so, rejoicing in my new freedom of motion and admiring the curves I made and my flowing drapery of white.

Freeing the Mind

BY TAKING OPIUM, people will not necessarily be transformed into gifted writers like Anderson and Coleridge. But through the experience of such dreams, opium does free the mind from some of its normal constraints, allowing incredible experiences. In this way, opium is like LSD, even though the overall effects of the drugs are quite different.

5
Early Use

THE USE OF OPIUM dates back further than written history. Archeological digs in Switzerland have found Opium Poppy seeds and pods, dating from the Neolithic age, a period running from 8000 BC to 5500 BC. This makes opium the oldest known drug, if in fact the people of that time were using it as a drug. It is possible that they were using poppies as a source food by eating the poppy seeds.

The Sumarians

THE FIRST PEOPLE known to have used opium are the Sumarians who lived in lower Mesopotamia, now western Iraq, in 3500 BC. The Sumarians are best remembered as the culture that invented writing. But in most ways, they were far ahead of their time. They produced ten times as much food as other farmers in the region—largely due to their use of irrigation. They traded extensively with their neighbors, especially food, opium, and beer. It is estimated that as much as half of the Sumarian barley crop went to beer production.

The Sumarians used opium medicinally. Some historians contend that opium was not used recreationally. This is highly unlikely since the Sumarian name for the opium poppy is *hul gil,* which means "joy plant." The Sumerians' use and export of alcohol indicates that recreational use of drugs was as important to the people of that time as it is today.

Opium Migrated

THANKS TO THE TRADING TIES of the Sumarians with their neighbors, the secret of opium and how to produce it eventually traveled westward. By 1300 BC, the Egyptians were cultivating poppies for the production of opium. The opium they produced was an extremely popular commodity. They traded it as far away as Greece and central Europe.

Opium was first used in the Middle East.

The first mention of opium by the Greeks was made around 330 BC by Hippocrates, the father of medicine. He wrote about opium's usefulness in curing a number of diseases, especially diarrhea. Later, around 150 BC, another Greek physician, Galen, took up opium as a kind of cause. Even though he is credited with writing the first description of an opium overdose, he still advocated its use for a number of medical purposes.

Dioscorides made the last real Greek investigation of opium in the 1st Century AD. His analysis is as valid today as it was then. He noted that it was highly effective at relieving nausea, diarrhea, and insomnia, as well as being used as an aphrodisiac.

Opium has a much greater association with the Far East than it does with the West. People often assume that opium originated in the East and was exported to the West, part of the so-called "yellow menace." This, however, seems not to be the case. Opium was first produced in the Middle East, then used in Europe and moved southeast to Mesopotamia. It was only after opium was being produced in Egypt and Europe that it was exported to the Far East.

At around 330 BC, Alexander the Great introduced opium to Persia. This was not the first time that opium had been sent to Persia, however. Some 3000 years earlier, the Sumarians were trading opium there. With the decline of the Sumarians, however, opium stopped being imported. As a result, opium vanished from Persian culture. So when Alexander brought it there, it was a new commodity. Seven-hundred years later, opium finally arrived in China. The opium came from Egypt by way of Arab traders.

Smoking Opium

FOR THE FIRST 1000 YEARS opium was used in China, it was primarily drunk. It was the Dutch who began the practice of combining opium with tobacco and smoking it in a pipe. This happened around 1500. This practice caught on quickly among the Chinese after having been introduced to it by the Portuguese, about 200 years later.

The practice of smoking opium mixed with tobacco did not stay in use for long. The Chinese gave it up in favor of the direct vaporization technique, which is still the most widely used by smokers today.

Laudanum

LAUDANUM was invented in 1527, around the same time the Dutch began smoking opium. Although laudanum can contain many different ingredients, its most basic form is opium dissolved in alcohol. The most famous of these was Sydenham's Laudanum, which was a combination of sherry and opium. The sweetness of the sherry made the bitter taste of the opium more palatable. For the next 400 years, laudanum was the most popular form of opium in the West.

Imported into China

OVER THE NEXT FEW CENTURIES we see an increase in the export of opium from Europe into China. The commodity the British most wanted from China was tea. About the only thing the Chinese wanted from the Europeans was opium. The Chinese grew their own opium poppies, but they were not very successful at it. As a result, they did not produce nearly enough opium to satisfy their own market. In addition, the Chinese opium was of a low quality that was little coveted.

Even though the Portuguese and Dutch had been big importers of opium to China, by 1800 England had a near monopoly on opium imported to the region. The East India Company was responsible for this export, but they were so involved with the British government by the time of the Opium Wars, that it doesn't make sense to talk about the opium traders as anything but English.

Business was booming. The market was growing almost every year due to a number of causes. First, the population of China was increasing rapidly at this time— roughly doubling from 1750 to 1850. Second, the number of people taking opium was increasing. Third, the amount of opium people were consuming was increasing.

6
Opium Wars

THE CHINESE GOVERNMENT HAD MADE OPIUM importation illegal in 1796. Actually, the sale of opium had already been nominally illegal for almost a hundred years before that— though tariffs were collected on these "illegal" sales. For the 40 years following 1796, the government again did little to enforce its new law. When the government did finally try to enforce the opium ban, it led to the two Opium Wars, although in fact they are pretty much just one war with a long cease-fire in the middle.

Today, it is fashionable to see the two Opium Wars as being a fight between the caring, paternal Chinese government, trying to save its people from the horror of opium addiction, and the greedy English, lining their pockets by making the Chinese people into virtual slaves.

This view—common though it is—is no more correct or objective than the view that new-world merchants where enslaving Europe with their export of coffee and tobacco.

Trade Deficit

THE FACTS ARE that the Chinese government was concerned about one thing—its large trade deficit with England. No country likes to have large trade deficits, because it means that the wealth of the country is being moved to another country, especially when exchanged for an ephemeral product like food or drugs. It is true that the Chinese government made opium smoking illegal much earlier than the 1796 law. This was based mostly on hysterical fears— "Opium smoking makes the face shrivel up." The government did nothing to stop opium from coming into the country, until it became economically un-pleasant to lose so much of the country's wealth. During all this time, the Chinese government had no problem with the use of the poor-quality opium that China was producing.

On the other side, the English were not forcing the Chinese to take their opium. A small fraction of the Chinese people wanted opium, and their voices were heard through the market when they bought it. The vast majority of Chinese people didn't want opium, and didn't buy it.

Slavery

ROUGHLY TWO CENTURIES before the Opium Wars, European governments banned the im-port of silk from Asia because of the trade deficits it was causing. This was the primary reason that the East India Company changed from distrib-uting silk to opium. However, no one accuses the English of enslaving Europe over silk. Why? Because the Europeans wanted the silk. Similarly, the Chinese wanted opium.

One little mentioned aspect of the whole 19ᵗʰ Century opium trade debate is that the opium going to China was from India. It is said that England enslaved China with opium. Actually England enslaved India and made the people produce opium at ridiculously low wages. They did this with guns which are the only effective tool for enslavement. India was enslaved with guns, China was *not* enslaved with opium.

The Wars

THE FIRST OPIUM WAR started due to the seizure of 95 tons of opium from British merchant ships. China was simply enforcing a law that it had created but not enforced for almost 50 years. Just the same, it looked very much like simple theft to the English given that England had been doing this business for the previous 50 years.

Britain won the war in 1842. But the Chinese government never really complied with the ambiguous terms of the surrender treaty. As a result, hostilities resumed in 1856 over an incident very much like the one that started the first Opium War—seizing a ship's cargo and charging its crew with drug smuggling. The Chinese government finally admitted defeat in 1860.

Do not assume that all opium users are addicts.

The end result of the two Opium Wars was that the Chinese people were allowed to buy good quality opium, imported from India. Opium use and addiction continued to increase for the rest of the 19ᵗʰ Century. But these rates where only comparable to the rates that existed after opium importation by the English was stopped in the early 20ᵗʰ Century. Their use was small compared to the use rates for other drugs such as alcohol, nicotine, and caffeine—then or now.

Hysteria

AT THE END OF THE FIRST OPIUM WAR, the opium addiction rate was extremely low—less than 1%. Even at the turn of the 20th Century, when opium imports were stopping, the addiction rate was only 3.4%. A widely quoted figure is that 27% of the adult male population of China were opium smokers in 1906. This statistic is usually quoted with addiction statistics, implying that the 27% were addicts. Most people automatically assume that opium users are addicts; this is not true, however. As we know from heroin use in the United States, roughly five times as many people have tried heroin as are addicted to it. Applying this conservative estimate to the Chinese numbers, we estimate that only 5% of these men were addicts.

This confusion is typical of the hysteria producing propaganda from people against drug-freedom, who assert that all humans will become addicted to drugs if they are legal. Our shared experiences with alcohol, cigarettes, and caffeine contradict this idea. Unfortunately most people believe that the legal status of a drug indicates its dangerousness. For two years in the United States, heroin was legal and alcohol was illegal. Did something change about these two drugs? No. It just means that drug laws are created for reasons that have little to do with the effects of the drugs themselves—reasons that change with the political winds.

It is hard to compare this number to modern China, because for years the communist government made China isolated from most other countries. Little food, as well as opium, was imported. As a result, opium addition stayed very low, just as hunger stayed high. As China became involved in global legal commerce, the opium started flowing in and the addicts started piling up.

7
Death of Opium

WHILE ALL OF THE POLITICAL MACHINATIONS were ensuing in Asia, Friedrich Setuerner was doing work in his laboratory that would change the world forever. He isolated the drug found in highest abundance in opium—morphine, named after Morpheus, the Greek god of sleep. It turns out that morphine is also responsible for the majority of the opium effect—especially for the euphoria and dream-like state it creates.

Modern Pharmocology

ISOLATING MORPHINE MARKED THE BEGINNING of modern pharmacology. Science began investigating all of the natural drugs to see what was inside them. This has been done more to opium than to any other drug. Since Seturner's work, scientists have isolated over fifty distinct alkaloids in opium. And the search continues.

The isolation of morphine brought about a change in the way medicine was used. Doctors and patients alike expected drugs to be very specific in their actions. In western countries, drugs like opium are rarely prescribed. Instead, one particular compound from opium is given to a patient, usually in pill form.

Banned

THE BEGINNING OF THE 20ᵀᴴ CENTURY saw most countries creating laws that banned the use of opium.
The United States banned opium for a number of
reasons. Probably the most important, at the federal
level, was that the government wanted to cozy up to
China in order to gain access to its lucrative markets.
Sound familiar?

At the local level, opium was banned because of
its association with the Chinese. In fact, many of the
early laws banned opium use by the Chinese, while
whites were exempt. This kind of racism was responsible for much of the global pressure to make drugs
illegal. It was formalized in the Eugenic movement.

The Eugenic Movement

THE IDEA BEHIND this movement was to make human
bloodlines stronger by, among other measures, keeping
them free of impurities. The banning of drugs was
supposed to create better humans
because drugs "dirtied" the body and
the soul. Eugenicists saw the phrase
"cleanliness is next to godliness" as
discouraging the listener from soiling
his body with alcohol and other
"pollutants"—*not* as encouraging
regular bathing.

> The Eugenics
> Movement
> killed opium.

According to this movement, a big part of this
"pollution" existed because different races inter-bred.
The global Eugenics movement gave us the Nazis, the
Drug War, and Narcotics Anonymous where people
proudly announce how long their bodies have been
"clean." Hitler was favorably inclined towards the
United States largely because of the history of the
Eugenics movement there.

Freedom is Slavery

A COMMON MESSAGE found in Nazi concentration camps at the beginning of World War II proclaimed, "There is a road to freedom. Its milestones are Obedience, Endeavor, Honesty, Order, Cleanliness, Sobriety, Truthfulness, Sacrifice, and love of the Fatherland." The message was signed by Adolf Hitler, but it could just as easily have come from any modern day politician, such as John F. Kennedy or Ronald Reagan. George Orwell put it most bluntly: "Freedom is slavery."

The Eugenics Movement saw its greatest triumph in the creation of drug laws that had not existed outside of religious rule. It basically stopped the use of opium anywhere except right near the source. But the ban did not work in the way the idealists had wanted. When opium became illegal, distributors needed to limit their risk. As a result, they increased the potency of their product. Out went opium and in came heroin.

Illegal commodities are sold in their most concentrated forms. Today, most alcohol is distributed as beer and wine. During prohibition—when it was illegal—alcohol was distributed as whisky. So today, most illegal inter-country distribution of opium is heroin. Heroin is a slight chemical alteration of morphine, the most active of opium's many active ingredients. Heroin is much more potent than opium. In addition, since heroin is very expensive, users commonly inject the drug right into a vein rather than simply drinking or smoking it. So society trades opium smokers for heroin injectors.

Misguided Regulation

GOVERNMENTS OF THE WORLD, in trying to solve one problem, commonly created a much bigger problem. Today, there are more addicts as a percent than there were before drug prohibition. Since they inject their drugs, there are more sudden deaths and diseases spread. Since the cost is high, many addicts resort to crime to acquire the money they need to buy their drugs. The laws have made what problems there were much worse.

Productivity Boost

THERE IS A STRONG TENDENCY to make the unstated assumption that addiction is harmful in and of itself. This assumption is untrue. Addiction is not necessarily harmful when the drug in question is legal, readily available, and cheap. Alcohol is an example. Under such circumstances, addicts are usually able to lead normal and productive lives. With alcohol we call these people "social drinkers."

In some cases, addiction can even be helpful. Caffine is a good example. Coffee drinking is normally associated with higher employee productivity in corporate environments. In fact, there is much evidence that indicates that the increase in stimulant and depressant use during the 19th Century was caused by changes in the work environment. Before the industrial revolution, people were allowed to work as their bodies dictated. With industrialization, people were expected to work specific times. Thus, they needed stimulants to get them going in the morning and depressants to make them relax at night.

Using opium made hard work easier to take.

The Chinese immigrants who helped build the intercontinental railroad where known for their high level of productivity, which was attributed to opium use. Using opium allowed them to bear the physical pain and mental boredom of the job. It is likely that the difficult aspects of the job promoted using opium.

In 1900, the Chinese were the most hated ethnic group in the United States. Samuel Gompers, as president of the

American Federation of Labor, attacked the Chinese systematically and continually through the second half of the 19ᵗʰ Century for being bad workers because of their opium smoking. This was, of course, complete fiction. First the Chinese were exceptional workers. Second, most Chinese immigrants were not opium users. And third, opium helped those who used it work well under terrible conditions. Gompers real reason for vilifying the Chinese was that they posed a threat to the members of his union.

Controversy Continues

WITHOUT THE LICIT OPIUM TRADE, and its supply of morphine, codeine, and thebaine, the world would be dependent upon the pure synthetic opioids. The choice for pain relief would be inferior and more expensive than using the natural source of these chemicals. Some have suggested this as a measure to curb "drug abuse." If such a measure did reduce heroin use, people who use heroin would most likely switch to more potent synthetics, such as Fentanyl and its analogs which are anywhere from 30 to 1000 times as strong as heroin. This policy would likely have little effect, however, given that most illegal heroin comes from illegally grown poppies. If such a policy were enacted, the only possible consequence would be negative.

The human culture that traveled to the moon is the same one that has been ingesting opium alkaloids for thousands of years. No major harm has come to this culture; the alkaloids have been tested. This cannot be said of the next test-tube miracle. Narcotics without opium are like clouds without rain.

8
Chemistry

OPIUM HAS A PROFOUND EFFECT on humans because the chemicals in opium mimic many of the most important chemicals found in the human body. It also changes the way that the body produces its own chemicals.

Most of the research on how opium affects the human body's central nervous system or CNS, has been focused on morphine, because it is by far the most abundant element found in opium. Morphene is responsible for the primary effects of opium and it has the most medicinal uses. Looking at just one part of opium gives the wrong idea about how the CNS, as well as opium, works. The chemicals that are found inside opium do all kinds of things and make the experience of opium distinctly richer than morphine.

Multiple Chemicals, Many Effects

THE OPIUM ALKALOIDS vary greatly in their effects. One alkaloid stimulates a GABA-receptor—the receptors associated with benzodiazepines such as Valium® and Xanax®. This is the receptor that alcohol and Valium® effect. Another alkaloid stimulates the adrenaline receptor. So opium gets you coming and going. Other alkaloids counter each other more directly. For example, some stimulate dopamine release while others block it. Similarly, one alkaloid potentiates the morphine histamine release, while another diminishes it. The result of all these different effects is to make opium a complex substance that is far from giving up all its secrets.

With the information we have available, it is difficult to say how opium affects the CNS. By looking at the way the system works, however, combined with some of the ways opium affects the system elements, we can get a better idea of the chemical basis for the rich opium experience.

Chemical Messages

WHEN WE FEEL HAPPY, it is because there are chemicals in our brains telling us to feel that way. There is an elaborate system of such chemicals, called *neurotransmitters*, which are created by the body. There are also corresponding receptors to which the chemicals attach. When the receptor is activated by the attachment of one of these neurotransmitters, it causes the body to do something depending upon the receptor. The messages vary widely. They can tell the body to feel a certain way, like relaxed; or they can tell the body to do something, like create a particular enzyme.

Neurotransmitters and receptors are a fundamental part of the nervous system. They allow the nervous system to communicate with itself and the rest of the body. A good way to think of how the CNS communicates with an organ is to imagine the organ having a bunch of buttons on it, like an old car radio. The button pushed determines what the organ will do. The buttons are like the receptors, and which one is pushed is determined by the neurotransmitter

Brain chemicals tells us to feel happy or sad.

that the nervous system sends. Any given neurotransmitter can only activate one receptor, or push one button—in theory anyway.

Actually, neurotransmitters are not so specific. This is particularly true of the endorphins. As we will see, morphine—the chemical that binds to the receptors designed for the endorphins—seems to push all the buttons. Morphine does, however, like some buttons more than others.

Five neurotransmitters are known to be important to the effect that opium has on the body: dopamine, epinephrin, norepinephrin, acetylcholine, and serotonin. Endorphins are also neurotransmitters, but they are not important to the effects of opium, because morphine takes their place. However, understanding endorphins helps understand morphine, so we will discuss them separately.

Dopamine

DOPAMINE is basically a stimulating agent. People with high levels of dopamine are usually exuberant and outgoing. It affects the part of the brain that controls movement, emotional response, and sensory experience—both pleasurable and painful.

Dopamine is an integral part of the body's reward system.

Most important to our understanding of opium is that dopamine is an integral part of the body's reward system. The body's release of dopamine is pleasant.

Opium stimulates the effects of dopamine in two major ways. This increased dopamine effect *should* make opium a stimulate, and it would, if there were nothing more to opium. Other properties of opium more than counter the dopamine-created effects.

Epinephrin and Norepinephrin

LIKE DOPAMINE, epinephrin and norepinephrin stimulate the body. In this case, they stimulate muscle tissue. Epinephrin stimulates striated muscles, which are the muscles under conscious control, like those in the legs and arms. Norepinephrin stimulates smooth muscles, like the heart and diaphragm. Under normal circumstances, the main purpose of norepinephrin is to keep blood pressure from getting too low. Opium counters the effects of both epinephrin and norepinephrin to relax muscles and reduce respiration.

Acetylcholine

ACETYLCHOLINE IS THE MOST ABUNDANT NEUROTRANSMITTER in the body. It is responsible for muscle contraction, but its broader effect is to relax the body. Opium decreases the release of acetylcholine. This is one of the ways that opium increases the dopamine effect. Acetylcholine counters the effect of dopamine, so if there is less acetylcholine, there will be more dopamine.

Serotonin

SEROTONIN INHIBITS ACTIVITY BY THE BODY. It is important to the autonomic nervous system in two ways relative to opium. First, serotonin counters norepinephrin in the same way that acetylcholine counters dopamine. Second, serotonin causes the release of endorphins from the spinal cord. It appears that opium increases the amount of serotonin in the body.

Agonists and Antagonists

NEUROCHEMICALS MUST PERFORM TWO FUNCTIONS to transmit the message they are designed to communicate. First, they must bind to the receptor site. Second, they must activate the receptor site. Any chemical that performs both these functions is called an agonist of that receptor. Some chemicals only perform the first function, however. They bind to the site, but don't activate it. This means that the receptor is blocked without performing its function. Chemicals that do this are called antagonists.

To make matters even more complicated, there are chemicals known as agonist-antagonists. The net effect of such chemicals is that the receptor is activated, but not to the maximum level. We can think of this like a light dimmer: turned all the way on, it is like a pure agonist; turned all the way off, it is like a pure antagonist; and in between are all the mixed agonist-antagonists. From this example, we can see that some agonist-antagonists are predominantly agonists, while others are largely antagonists.

It is not known exactly what makes a chemical an agonist-antagonist. Agonist-antagonists could exhibit their behavior by binding to the receptor, but activating it poorly. This is the most direct explanation. On the other hand, an individual agonist-antagonist molecule may work as a full agonist at a receptor site when it fits in one way, but work as a full antagonist when it fits in another way. When many such molecules are present, the effect will be mixed with some agonist action and some antagonist action. In addition to these theories, agonist-antagonists could work in a number of other ways—some of which are already theorized while others are waiting to be discovered.

The Nervous System

THE NERVOUS SYSTEM IS DIVIDED INTO TWO PARTS. The part of the nervous system under conscious control is called the somatic nervous system. The higher brain controls this system, and so it is not terribly relevant to understanding opium. The other part of the nervous system is under unconscious or automatic control. This is called the autonomic nervous system.

Autonomic Nervous System

THE AUTONOMIC NERVOUS SYSTEM is divided into two parts: sympathetic and parasympathetic. These two parts have opposite effects. The sympathetic portion causes the body to become excited. For example, it would be responsible for increasing respiration. The parasympathetic portion causes the body to become relaxed. For example, it would be responsible for lowering blood pressure. These subsystems help the body maintain biological equilibrium, or homeostasis, because they counter the effects of each other.

Sympathetic System

THE SYMPATHETIC SYSTEM is responsible for the "fight or flight" response. When an object is suddenly moving quickly toward someone's face, heart rate and respiration increase and he becomes hyper-alert.

The sympathetic system gives us extra energy.

This is why people experience time moving more slowly than usual during accidents. These reactions take place automatically, to bypass the higher functions of the brain and work through the more primitive brain stem. The sympathetic portion of the autonomic nervous system works primarily by releasing neurotransmitters, the most important of which are norepinephrin and dopamine.

Many functions of the body are under this type of control. Heart rate and breathing are examples. Breathing is the only part of the autonomic nervous system under conscious control. Autonomic breathing is regulated as a response to carbon dioxide levels within the body. Conscious breathing is regulated by an act of will, but there is a limit to this. Breathing too much or too little will cause the body to lose consciousness and the autonomic system will take over. Breathing is controlled primarily by the autonomic nervous system. It is a finely tuned response system imperative for survival.

When stimulated, the sympathetic system gives extra energy to the human, sometimes allowing him to do the impossible. For example, it can allow someone to have extraordinary strength by shunting blood away from the internal organs to the skeletal system. For short periods of time, this sort of excessive stimulation of parts of the body is extremely important. For long periods of time, however, such activation damages the body.

Parasympathetic System

THE PARASYMPATHETIC PORTION of the autonomic nervous system is responsible for mediating the sympathetic subsystem. Its response and stimulation is the direct opposite of the sympathetic portion of the autonomic nervous system. Thus, the parasympathetic system lowers heart rate, blood pressure, and respiration. It achieves these effects by causing the release of acetylcholine and serotonin, which counter the effects of the neurotransmitters released by the sympathetic portion.

Opioid Receptors

OPIOID RECEPTORS EXIST throughout the body, but most are located within the CNS—the brain and spinal cord. There are also opioid receptors in the intestines, which is why opioids are constipating agents. The body has three classifications of receptors. It is almost certain that more will be found. The function of these sites is only moderately understood.

Mu Receptors

WHEN THE MU RECEPTORS are activated, they produce a number of effects: analgesia, drowsiness, constipation, nausea, itching, pupil constriction, confusion, euphoria and respiratory depression. They are located around the spinal cord, moving up to the brain stem and into the midbrain. It is believed, thus far, that there are two kinds of mu receptors: mu-1 and mu-2. Mu-1 receptors modulate analgesia and euphoria, while mu-2 receptors modulate respiratory depression.

These two mu receptors present a bit of hope that drugs can be developed that will effectively treat pain in people who are already addicted to opioids, such as terminal cancer patients using opioids to manage the pain. With morphine, which fills both mu receptors, analgesia will necessarily go along with respiratory depression. If a specific agonist for the mu-1 receptor could be created, however, pain could be modulated without reducing respiration and risking death. A better drug would be a mu-1 agonist and mu-2 antagonist.

Other Receptors

MORPHINE AND ALL OF THE PURE AGONIST opioids bind to the mu receptors far more than they do to the others. Currently, there are two other receptors: kappa and delta. Kappa receptors produce fewer effects when they are activated than do mu receptors. These include analgesia, minor respiratory depression, and minor pupil constriction. The kappa receptors also produce dysphoria—a feeling of discomfort and unhappiness. Most of the drugs that activate the kappa receptors antagonize the mu receptor. As a result, we think of the kappa receptor as causing dysphoria when this is, in fact, an indirect effect. When all the mu receptors are filled, opioids will fill the Kappa receptors. This is why opium use can cause depression in addicts. Delta receptors are poorly understood, but they seem to act much like the mu receptors.

The GABA Connection

GABA RECEPTORS ARE to benzodiazepines and barbiturates, what opioid receptors are to morphine. When GABA receptors are stimulated, they slow the body down. One of the ways they do this is by stopping dopamine from traveling through the nervous system. When an opioid receptor is stimulated, it can shut down nearby GABA receptors. As a result, dopamine is increased. But as we have noted, at least one opium component stimulates GABA receptors. This is another example of the complexity of opium interaction.

Endorphins

WHEN ENDORPHINS WERE FIRST DISCOVERED, it was thought that there was just one—the body's internal morphine. But as time went on, more and more endorphins popped up. Like morphine, they all fit into and activate at least one opioid receptor. Chemically, however, endorphins are nothing like morphine. Morphine has a clumped structure to it, whereas endorphins are long chains of atoms. And morphine is small. The first endorphin discovered was also the smallest—met-enkephalin. This smallest endorphin is still more than twice as massive as morphine.

Endorphins help account for opiums feel-good effects.

Beta-Endorphin

THE BETA-ENDORPHIN IS THE MOST POTENT of the endorphins. It is almost 50 times as strong as morphine when the two drugs are put directly into the brain. It is a very large molecule, however, which has a hard time working its way from the bloodstream into the brain. Even so, when put into the body intravenously, it is still three times as potent as morphine.

The beta-endorphin is released in the bodies of pregnant women in increasing amounts until the baby is born. Within two days of birth, they are gone from the mother's body. It is believed they are created for the benefit of the fetus—to retard or completely inhibit breathing. The corresponding sedation of the fetus protects the mother by preventing large amounts of fetal activity, which might injure her.

The beta-endorphin may be most important to the fetus, but it still has a profound effect on the mother. It may account for the good feeling most women experience during pregnancy and may affect general pain perception. Given this information, it is possible that postpartum depression is due to withdrawal from this kind of endorphin.

Pleasure or Pain?

PEOPLE USUALLY THINK of endorphins as chemicals that
control mood. Since all the opioid receptor sites do
something to modulate pain, however, we might beg the
question, "Are endorphins pain relieving chemicals rather
than pleasure producing chemi-
cals?" More and more, it looks

Like morphine, like the feelings of euphoria that
endorphins fit into go along with them are an evolu-
opioid receptors. tionary adaptation to pain. We
can better deal with pain when we
are happy. Endorphins are released when the body is
strained and in pain—*not when it is unhappy.* It is more
accurate to call endorphins the body's "pain relievers"
than the body's euphoriants.

Mixing Things Up

THE CENTRAL NERVOUS SYSTEM is a complicated machine
with all kinds of feedback mechanisms pushing and
pulling the body in different directions. The same can
be said of the "opium machine." When opium is
introduced into the brain, the brain's chemical mixture
is disturbed dramatically. But the brain is accustomed to
this. Opium effects the CNS by playing by the rules of
the CNS itself, but in a fanciful and extreme manner.
Like any drug, opium changes the rate at which the
body is doing the things it already does. It doesn't
make it do things it doesn't otherwise do.

9
Major Constituents

ROUGHLY THREE-QUARTERS OF WHAT OPIUM is made up of is chemically uninteresting: water, sugars, proteins, ammonia, latex, gums, plant wax, fats, and sulfuric, lactic, and meconic acid. The other one-quarter of opium has had scientists digging deeper and deeper into opium, looking for yet another "active ingredient," which may have some therapeutic use. These active ingredients are called alkaloids.

Alkaloids

THERE ARE A LOT OF ALKALOIDS in opium, although the exact number is hard to nail down. Most sources say that more than 20 alkaloids have been isolated from opium. Some reports go as high as 50. It is unclear if all the alkaloids are present in all opium samples, however. One thing is certain—the number of known alkaloids is increasing.

The five most abundant alkaloids are listed in the table below. It is clear from this table that the remaining opium constituents must be found at very low levels. There are two reasons for this. First, the smaller quantity compounds—codeine, papaverine, and thebaine—are present at about the 1% level, so the other alkaloids would have to be present at even lower levels. Second, the five most abundant chemicals make up 24% of the weight of opium, on average. That doesn't leave much room for the other alkaloids, since all the alkaloids in opium combined comprise only about 25% of opium by weight.

Although there isn't much room left for the remaining opium alkaloids, many of them are very interesting, and they don't need to be found in high abundance to add to the overall effect of opium. In addition, many may be useful in creating new drugs that address certain ailments.

Major Constituents of Opium

Alkaloid	Chemical Class	Abundance
Morphine	Phenanthrene	10-15%
Noscapine	Benzylisoquinolines	4-8%
Codeine	Phenanthrene	1-3%
Papaverine	Benzylisoquinolines	1-3%
Thebaine	Phenanthrene	1-2%

Alkaloid Classes

THE ALKALOIDS IN OPIUM fall into one of two chemical classes: phenanthrenes and benzylisoquinolines. The two classes are distinguished by their structure. The benzylisoquinolines are characterized by having a couple of benzyl groups. This causes such compounds to be elongated because two benzene rings are attached by a string of two hydrogen atoms. Phenanthrenes, in contrast, have a condensed structure where the benzene groups are butted up against each other. So in the simplest terms, benzylisoquinolines are

Benzene Ring

long chain-like chemicals and phenanthrenes are compact clumps. Both classes are actually part of the isoquinoline group of chemicals, which is two benzene rings with one of the carbon atoms replaced with a nitrogen. The phenanthrenes are created from the benzylisoquinolines, with the

Isoquinoline latter folding in on themselves and creating the former.

Opioids

OF ALL OF THE FIFTY OR MORE opium alkaloids, only two are what are called *opioids*—chemicals that act at the opioid receptor sites in the human body. These opioids are morphine and codeine. Codeine does not activate the opioid receptors directly. It does so indirectly by transforming into morphine. But saying that codeine is not an opioid would also mean we would have to say that heroin is not an opioid. It is far too confusing. Drugs that readily metabolize into opioids are opioids. The other alkaloids have effects, but they are not responsible for the dreamy euphoria for which opium is known. Part of this effect is to make opium a more pleasant and less toxic drug than either of the naturally occurring opioids are when taken alone.

Morphine

MEDICINALLY, opium has three primary uses: it is an excellen pain reliever, cough suppressar and diarrhea cure. The constit of opium that eases pain to t greatest degree is morphine.

Morphine is the most effective chemical in opium for reducing coughs and

Morphine

relieving diarrhea. Because of its greater potential for addiction, other drugs, such as the more toxic codeine, are used in preference to morphine. In fact, most of the legal morphine produced is used to create codeine because the medical demand for morphine is roughly the same as for codeine. The supply of morphine, however, is greater, with opium containing roughly five times as much morphine as codeine.

Noscapine

NOSCAPINE HAS NO NARCOTIC PROPERTIES. The only commercial use it has found is as a cough suppressant. Sources disagree as to how good a cough suppressant it is. Some say that it is better than codeine and other say that it is worse than dextromethorphan, an over-the-counter cough suppressant. Noscapine is a weak smooth muscle relaxant, analgesic, and sedative. In other words, it is an effective, albeit mild, therapeutic drug.

Codeine

CODEINE IS AN EXCELLENT cough suppressant and is sold over-the-counter in many countries. Codeine does not, however, relieve pain. This may come as a surprise to many readers because codeine is commonly prescribed for pain, especially for dental pain. For most people, codeine relieves pain indirectly because about 10% of it metabolizes into morphine. For others, codeine relieves no pain at all, either directly or indirectly.

Pure codeine is Schedule II under federal law, indicating that it has a high potential for abuse. Despite this governmental scheduling, codeine actually has a relatively low potential for physical addition. Withdrawal from codeine is not nearly as difficult as withdrawal from morphine. On the other hand, it is much easier to overdose on codeine. Unlike most opioid overdoses, which are due to respiratory depression, codeine causes fluids to fill the lungs, called pulmonary edema, which drowns the victim.

Papaverine

Papaverine

PAPAVERINE IS A SMOOTH MUSCLE RELAXANT. Like almost everything else in opium, has no narcotic properties. One of the most successful uses of Papaverine has been in the treatment of male impotence. Small amounts of this drug injected into the base of the penis have a startlingly effective in producing penis erections.

Thebaine

THEBAINE HAS A CHEMICAL STRUCTURE that is almost identical to that of morphine and codeine, but has no narcotic properties. In small doses, its primary effect is nausea and in large doses it brings on strychnine-like convulsions. Because of its structural similarity to the natural opioids, however, thebaine is used extensively in the pharmaceutical industry to create synthetic and semi-synthetic opioids.

The United States government has considered using Oriental Poppies, *Papaver bracteatum* and *Papaver orientale,* to supply the pharmaceutical industry's need for opium, because these poppies produce little or no morphine but decent amounts of thebaine. There is little worry that this form of opium would be diverted to the illicit market, since the illicit market is only interested in morphine for conversion into heroin. The thebaine could then be used to create the semi-synthetic opioids as well as codeine, which are normally created from morphine.

10
Minor Constituents

No plant has been picked over like the opium poppy. Starting in 1803 when Hans Sertürner isolated morphine from opium, scientists have been busy isolating other compounds and studying their effects. Although none of the subsequent chemicals has turned out to be as generally useful as morphine, many are still quite useful. Regardless, they all add to the complex chemical soup, which is opium.

Below is a list of the opium constituents that have been studied, along with what is known about them. This list is certainly not comprehensive. Compounds from opium continue to be isolated to this day, in an effort to find new, useful drugs.

Alpha-Allocryptopine

Allocryptopine has a cornucopia of uses. It produces anti-arrhythmic—stabilizing an inconsistently beating heart local anesthetic, and anti-bacterial effects. In addition, there are indications that it inhibits tumor growth.

Berberine

Traditionally, berberine has been used as an anti-pyretic, or fever reducer. It has other uses such as the treatment of diarrhea and inflammation, but how it interacts with opioids is its most interesting feature. Although it is not very toxic, it potentates the histamine mortality associated with morphine. It also inhibits the formation of DNA, RNA, lipids, and proteins. The inhibition of protein formation is very interesting in that much of the protein used by the body goes to form endorphins. There is less need for endorphin creation by people on opium since they get endorphin replacements from morphine.

Canadine

CANADINE IS A WEAK ANTI-BACTERIAL SUBSTANCE with some sedative properties. It is known to inhibit liver alcohol dehydrogenase.

Coptisine

COPTISINE EXHIBITS anti-bacterial and anti-inflammatory properties.

Corytuberine

CORYTUBERINE IS a nasty chemical. At low doses, it counteracts the pain-relieving effect of morphine. At high doses, it causes asphyxia during convulsive seizures. Corytuberine also causes hypotension.

Cryptopine

CRYPTOPINE IS AN ANTI-ARRHYTHMIC DRUG, lowering blood pressure, but it is not as good as allocryptopine.

Dihydrosanguinarine

DIHYDROSANGUINARINE IS SIMILAR to sanguinarine but less toxic.

Isoboldine

ISOBOLDINE IS A WEAK ANTI-MICROBIAL DRUG. It also has a high affinity for the alpha$_1$-adrenoreceptor.

Isocorypalmine

THE ONLY RESEARCH ON ISOCORYPALMINE has been done in-vitro, meaning in an artificial environment. These studies indicate that it should limit blood platelet "clumping."

Laudanine

A METABOLITE OF LAUDANOSINE, laudanine causes acceler-ated respiration when taken in small doses. To some extent, this will offset lowered respiration caused by other chemicals found in opium. In large doses, which are not found in opium, Laudanine can cause tetany, a condition causing muscle spasms.

Laudanosine

LAUDANOSINE HAS BEEN WIDELY STUDIED because it is a principle metabolite of atracurium, the muscle relaxant. It seems to be responsible for some of atracurium's unwanted effects. Laudanosine crosses the blood-brain barrier easily, where it can cause hypotension.

Magnofluorine

MAGNOFLUORINE IS AN ANTI-INFLAMMATORY, which lowers blood pressure. It also inhibits protein formation. Toxic levels cause respiratory failure.

Narceine

NARCEINE IS QUITE SIMILAR to codeine in its pharmacol-ogy. However, since it does not metabolize into mor-phine, it is missing any analgesic effect. In contrast to codeine, it increases respiration in terms of breath frequency and air volume.

Narcotoline

NARCOTOLINE IS a cough-suppressant, but not a particu-larly good one.

Neopine

AT LOW DOSES, NEOPINE acts very much like codeine except that it does not relieve pain, and it is less effective. It exhibits some narcotic effects but it is highly toxic.

Oripavine

ORIPAVINE IS ABOUT AS GOOD A PAIN RELIEVER as morphine. The problem is that it is far more toxic. At low doses, it causes tremors and vomiting. At high doses, it causes convulsions followed by death. It is cross-tolerant with morphine, which means that taking it will make morphine less effective. One of the most interesting aspects of this non-opioid is that prolonged use will cause dependence resulting in withdrawal very similar to morphine, but it has no effect on morphine withdrawal itself. The opposite seems to be the case, in fact. Oripavine is a weak antagonist of morphine—dislodging morphine from receptor sites without continuing to fulfill the role of morphine at the site.

Protopine

PROTOPINE IS A VERY EFFECTIVE ANTI-ARRHYTHMIA drug for certain kinds of anti-arrhythmia. It slows the heart rate, decreases blood pressure, and produces sedation. Protopine is also a good smooth-muscle relaxant, slightly weaker than papaverine. There is some indication that Protopine may help prevent the fatal histamine release associated with large morphine doses.

Pseudomorphine

THIS ALKALOID HAS ALMOST NO EFFECT unless it is administered via intravenous injection. The problem is that Pseudomorphine is hardly soluble in water. Even small doses administered intravenously have a large effect, however. The most profound effect of Pseudomorphine is reduced blood pressure. It is possibly a morphine antagonist, even though Pseudomorphine is a metabolite of morphine.

Reticuline

RETICULINE SEEMS TO INHIBIT DOPAMINE from binding to certain receptor sites, so in this way it is a kind of weak dopamine antagonist. It also seems to block stimulants from effecting the body.

Rhoeadine

RHOEADINE IS A LARGE CONSTITUENT of the Opium Poppy's cousin, the Corn Poppy. It is a mild sedative.

Saguinarine

SAGUINARINE HAS A NUMBER OF USES. It increases blood pressure, muscle tone, and intestinal peristalsis. It is a good anti-microbial medication with a low toxicity. It seems to slow tumor growth. And perhaps most strange of all, it fights tooth decay by destroying plaque.

Salutaridine

SALUTARIDINE IS NOT A WELL-STUDIED CHEMICAL. The most notable thing about it is that it has a small tendency to stimulate the GABA receptors.

Scoulerine

SCOULERINE IS a sedative. It attaches to dopamine receptors in the brain.

Stepholidine

STEPHOLIDINE IS AN EXCITING DRUG from a medical perspective. It seems to be an effective analgesic and pyretic, with no tolerance and no withdrawal. It also lowers blood pressure.

Synergy

CHEMICALS THAT MAKE UP OPIUM have both positive and negative reinforcing effects. This causes opium to have a very complex nature, because even the effects that reinforce do so by different mechanisms. Overall, it is believed that opium is a safer drug than any of its isolated compounds. In particular, it is less likely to cause nausea and overdose than equivalent doses of morphine.

11
Morphine

THE EFFECTS OF OPIUM, either medically or recreationally, are defined in large part by morphine. Long before opium became simply the source of morphine, its quality was defined by its morphine content. No one paid more for opium with particularly high thebaine levels! This is because morphine has a very strong effect on the human body and it is present in opium at such a high level. Noscapine is the only opium constituent that is present at levels anywhere near that of morphine, and it is still only about one-third as abundant. In addition, roughly 10% of the codeine ingested by the human body is transformed into morphine.

Effects

WE TEND TO CREATE A FALSE DICHOTOMY when discussing the drug actions, by dividing them into medical effects and recreational effects. As a culture we have little moral problem with efforts to decrease pain. Efforts to increase happiness, however, are seen as sinful. What is happening in each case is an improvement in people's lives. By and large, the effects of morphine are to reduce pain or increase happiness—the two being the same thing.

State of Mind

THERE ARE THREE RELATED, but distinct feelings that morphine causes in a user: contentment, dreaminess, and relaxation.

Contentment

THE EARLIEST TERM FOR POPPIES translates as "joy plant." Joy is a pretty broadly defined word. The morphine joy is transcendental—it seems eternal. One has the feeling that happiness has been tapped without end. Many would capture this feeling in spiritual terms—at peace. In a western sense, it is best defined as "contented." Morphine makes the mind very focused on the present, without thought of the past or the future. Recall the 19th Century Chinese railroad workers in America who worked tirelessly without complaining.

The happiness caused by morphine is distinct from that caused by other drugs. LSD, for example, can make a person absolutely giddy with bouts of laughter. in con- define

hysterical Morphine is quiet, trast. One might the euphoria caused by LSD as extraverted, while morphine euphoria is introverted. Another distinct feeling associated with morphine is dreaminess.

Dreaminess

"OPIUM DREAMS" ARE DUE PRIMARILY to the morphine contained in opium. There are a few reasons why the effect is better when ingested as opium. First, it keeps the morphine dose low so that the dreamer is more lucid.

Second, some of the minor alkaloids found in opium modulate the dream- producing effect of morphine. Third, a large collection of alkaloids work-

Morphine joy is transcendental.

ing simultaneously on the brain cause its chemistry and, thus, its thinking to be more complex and convoluted. In addition to causing opium dreams, the morphine "high" has a dreamy quality to it. It is as though the right brain becomes more conscious without the left brain losing consciousness, as it does when sleeping. Associated with this are subtle visual and aural "imaginings" which are non-threatening and fit in with the emotional timbre of the experience.

Relaxation

MORPHINE GREATLY REDUCES ANXIETY. We discussed this effect when describing the nervous system and the effect of morphine on it. The part of the brain responsible for the "fight or flight" instinct is deadened, and so fewer alarm signals are sent out to the body. What this means in a subjective sense is that the user responds to outside stimulus more slowly and calmly.

Physical Discomfort

MANY OF THE ALKALOIDS in opium relieve pain, cough, and diarrhea. Morphine is about the most effective in relieving all of these discomforts, due to its greater concentration in opium.

Analgesia

THE PAIN-RELIEVING ABILITY OF MORPHINE is intimately linked to its mood-altering ability. Morphine decreases the strength of the pain signals that reach the brain as well as changing the way that the brain perceives pain. The pain is felt, but attitudes toward it change. The pain becomes unimportant.

Morphine is the constituent of opium that eases pain.

Morphine is primarily adminis-tered orally or intramuscularly, unless the patient is on an IV in a hospital. The normal dose for an adult male is about 15 mg, intramuscularly, every four hours. The dose is normally slightly higher when administered orally, but regardless, doses above 20 mg are rare.

Cough and Diarrhea

ALTHOUGH MORPHINE is an excellent reliever of cough and diarrhea, it is rarely prescribed as such. This is mostly due to concerns about addiction. In fact, the federal government questions prescription of morphine given for any use other than pain-relief for terminal patients.

Addiction

MORPHINE ADDICTION IS CONFINED PRIMARILY to the medical community because there really is not a black market in morphine. Most opioid addicts in the United States use heroin. From a chemical standpoint, heroin is morphine since heroin breaks done into morphine, and it is the morphine—not the heroin—that is responsible for the high. So when street addicts withdraw, they are with-drawing from morphine even though they are addicted to heroin.

Overdose

IT IS DIFFICULT, BUT POSSIBLE, to overdose on morphine. Morphine slows respiration and a large enough dose may cause breathing to stop all together. Other drugs taken with morphine, barbiturates for example, can potentate this effect and make overdoses more likely. Morphine, especially when administered intravenously, causes a sudden release of histamine in the brain, which can bring on cardiac arrest. Such effects would not be an overdose, technically, but the results would be the same.

12
Codeine

CODEINE HAS THE REPUTATION of being morphine's under-achieving sibling. It is true that in most ways, codeine does achieve less. This is true in almost all aspects of the drug's therapeutic uses, recreational uses, addiction potential, and withdrawal. But it is largely *because* codeine is less effective than morphine that it is a far more popular drug in the medical community. Codeine is so popular, in fact, that less than half of the morphine produced legally is used as morphine. Government intimidation of doctors has relegated morphine to use almost exclusively for terminal patients. With such a small demand, most of the morphine produced goes to make codeine.

The effects of codeine are quite similar to those of morphine with important differences. Even though it is usually thought to be less dangerous than morphine, this is only with regards to physical addiction. A much larger fraction of people are allergic to codeine than morphine, one reason why hydrocodone is increasingly used as a substitute for codeine. At an equivalent dose, codeine is far more toxic than morphine. Codeine has a better bioavailability when taken orally than morphine. Given that most morphine is converted to codeine, however, making the best use of these resources is clearly not a priority.

Pain Relief

ALTHOUGH CODEINE IS CLASSIFIED as a narcotic analgesic, it does not actually relieve pain. In terms of its analgesic effect, codeine is what is known as a pro-drug, or a substance that has no effect itself, but changes chemically into another substance that does have an effect. In this case, that chemically active substance is morphine. For most people, about 10% of the codeine ingested is transformed into morphine. Thus the usual levels at which codeine is prescribed for pain—15 mg to 60 mg—actually amount to about 1 mg to 5 mg of morphine.

Sparteine Oxygenase

IN ORDER FOR CODEINE to transform into morphine—and, thus, relieve pain—it must have access to a particular enzyme called sparteine oxygenase. Unfortunately, 7-10% of "white" humans have a genetic deficiency of this enzyme, making codeine no more than a placebo. This number is race dependent and has not been well studied. A similar effect takes place with hydrocodone—one of the drugs in Vicodin®. It owes its pain relieving ability to its transformation into hydromorphone, Dilaudid®.

7-10% of whites— 20 million people in the USA—don't respond to codine.

Doctors should be aware of this codeine-to-morphine transformation, and yet they are surprisingly ignorant on this matter. When patients complain that codeine, or hydrocodone, is not relieving their pain, they are not necessarily whining or trying to scam for more potent drugs. It may seem that 7% who don't respond is a small number, but this represents 20 million people in the United States alone—perhaps a half billion or more globally. That's 20 million people in the United States, for whom the most common treatment for mild to moderate pain is useless.

Drug & Food Interactions

SOME DRUGS WILL MAKE CODEINE less effective in reducing pain. The most important are the widely prescribed antidepressants known as SRIs, or Serotonin Reuptake Inhibitors. Paxil® and Prozac® are particularly bad in this regard.

Codeine itself will lower its conversion to morphine. This makes it a particularly bad drug for use in relieving pain over an extended period of time. Other substances lower the body's ability to absorb codeine. In particular, tannins found in many tart foods such as tea, wine, blackberries, and apples, can lower codeine absorption.

The body's conversion of codeine to morphine can be increased. The sleep-inducing drug gluthethimide is known to improve morphine yield percentages. As a result, the two drugs have been used together to detox and maintain heroin-addicted people.

Cough Suppression

AT LOW DOSES OF 5 MG TO 30 MG, codeine is used as an antitussive, or a cough suppressant. It acts on the central nervous system, raising the level of stimulus that the body needs to induce coughing. This is an effect of codeine itself and so codeine is effective at reducing coughs in all people. Other opioids are also useful in controlling coughs. Preparations containing hydrocodone or hydromorphone are available by prescription. Dextromethorphan, an opium derivative, is almost as good a cough suppressant as codeine. Even though it has similar side-effects, it is not a prescription item, most likely because it does not produce euphoria.

Anti-Diarrhea

LIKE MANY SUBSTANCES IN OPIUM, codeine is a constipating agent and thus an excellent treatment for diarrhea. The levels usually prescribed for this are roughly the same as when codeine is used as a cough suppressant: 5 mg to 30 mg. This aspect of codeine can be seen as an adverse effect, especially when codeine is taken over long periods of time. By ingesting large quantities of water, high-fiber food, and even laxatives, this problem can be ameliorated to some extent.

Euphoria

THE EUPHORIA ASSOCIATED with codeine comes primarily from its conversion to morphine. As a result, people who get little or no pain relief from codeine feel little euphoria as well. This is not surprising, given that much of morphine's pain-relieving ability stems from its ability to change the way the sufferer perceives the pain, rather than reducing the pain impulses that bombard the brain.

> *Euphoria associated with codeine comes from its conversion to morphine.*

Since most of the euphoria of codeine comes from its conversion to morphine, one might think that the codeine "high" would be the same as that of morphine, but it is not. Certainly, in a general sense, the feelings one experiences on codeine are similar, such as the dreamy, relaxed state. The codeine high is less pure than morphine, however. It is also not as rich and complex as opium.

People just beginning to experiment with codeine recreationally usually take whatever they happen to have, usually low doses of 15 mg or less. Experienced people can take very high doses of up to 250 mg. This is a dangerously high dose.

Other Effects

THERE ARE MANY OTHER EFFECTS associated with codeine, including lightheadedness, drowsiness, itchiness, urinary retention, or a difficulty in urinating, nausea, and vomiting. Whether they are good or bad is a matter of opinion and will vary depending upon the situation. For example, urinary retention might be a fine effect when one is suffering from dehydration, and some using codeine might find the "itch" pleasurable.

Addiction

MOST PEOPLE DON'T THINK OF CODEINE as being addictive, but it is, of course. Whether the addiction is to codeine, or the morphine it breaks down into, is unclear. Most likely it is both. Withdrawal symptoms seems like morphine, but at a low level. A codeine addiction of one gram per day would be equivalent to a 45 mg morphine habit or a 15 mg heroin habit taken intravenously. This is not much by modern standards, where "average" heroin addicts are doing at least 250 mg of heroin per day, which is roughly the same as 18 grams of codeine each day.

Overdose

CODEINE OVERDOSES CAN TAKE ON a number of forms, but two seem to predominate. First, there is the traditional opium overdose of reduced and eventual arrested breathing. This probably has something to do with the morphine that codeine is broken down into. The second form of overdose is pulmonary edema, which is an effect where the lungs fill with fluid and the victim effectively dies of drowning. This effect is especially associated with codeine that is administered intravenously. Codeine should only be administered intravenously by a professional, and never recreationally.

A similar death has been observed with users having what appear to be allergic reactions to oral doses of codeine as low as 500 mg. Codeine is a dangerous drug due to its high toxicity. Users who find their opioid tolerance increasing to the point where they need to take more than 200 mg of codeine should consider stopping.

The Soup

CODEINE DOES NOT ADD MUCH TO OPIUM. Its effects are weaker than morphine, but morphine is present in much higher concentrations. Codeine is important, however. It is an excellent medicine to use when morphine is deemed "too much." It is ingested very well orally, whereas morphine is poorly absorb when taken orally due to the liver's efficient removal of morphine. Most important, codeine is usually the first opioid that one experiences. It is an excellent indicator of how a person will respond to the more potent opioids. A person who really likes codeine may show poor restraint with more potent opioids, such as morphine or heroin.

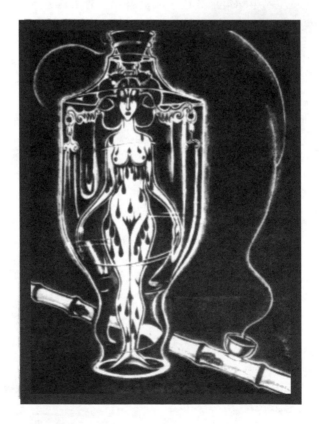

13

Poppy Classification

I<small>T IS SAID THAT THE</small> O<small>PIUM</small> P<small>OPPY</small> is a "true poppy," while the California Poppy is not. This confusion gives the impression that the California Poppy is misnamed. However, the fragile little flower is, indeed, part of the same botanical family as the Opium Poppy.

All plants belong to a particular family. One of those families is *Papaveraceae*, the Poppy family. This family is subdivided into subfamilies. Subfamilies are made up of a number of genera, which are further subdivided into species. Species are further divided into subspecies, or varieties. It is a system of classifying things that goes from the general to the specific.

Classification System

I. Family

A. Subfamily

1. Genus

a. Species

We could do the same with music. All music belongs to a particular type, or family–Blues, Jazz, Classical, or Rock. Each type can be further divided into periods, or subfamilies. For classical there are four:

Baroque, Classical, Romantic, and Modern. Each period can be divided into subperiods, or genera. For modern there are two: before World War II and after. The subperiods, or genera, can be divided into individual works, or species.

Poppy Subfamilies

NON-BOTANISTS TEND TO THINK in the *There are many species in the poppy family.* broadest or the narrowest terms about plants—families and species. This is how we get *California*, the species, *Poppy*, the family. Non-musicians tend to think in these terms, too. They can tell you if they like the classical music type and they can tell you if they like an individual work, like *Für Elise*, but not if they prefer the romantic period to the classical period.

The *Papaveraceae*, or Poppy, family is divided into four subfamilies: *chelidonioideae, eschscholzioideae, papaveroideae,* and *platystemonoideae*. It probably seems strange that the poppy family has a poppy subfamily. It's true, however, just like classical music has a classical period. Each of the subfamilies is divided into a number of genera. The *papaveroideae* subfamily has nine genera. As you might expect, one of those genera is also named "poppy," or *papaver*.

The True Poppy

WE ALL KNOW THE POPPY FAMILY, those poppies with brightly colored, flimsy looking flowers. We might know a few specific species in that family. The California Poppy is a species; the Himalayan Blue Poppy is a species; the Opium Poppy is a species. Let's use these as examples.

Almost all the flowers in the poppy family are called "poppies," but only those flowers that are in the poppy family, subfamily, and genus are called "true poppies." The California Poppy is in the poppy family, but it is in the *eschscholzioideae* subfamily, so it isn't a true poppy, it's a Californian Poppy. The Himalayan Blue Poppy is in the poppy family, *papaveroideae* is the subfamily, but the *Meconopsis* genus. So it isn't a true poppy, it's a Blue Poppy. Of the three poppies we mentioned above, only the Opium Poppy is in the *papaveraceae* family, *papaveroideae* subfamily, and *papaver* genus. Of these three poppies, only the opium poppy is a "true poppy."

There are roughly 250 species in the poppy family. The California, Himalayan Blue, and Opium Poppies are all in this family. There are 150 species in the poppy subfamily. The Himalayan Blue and Opium Poppies are in this subfamily. Seventy species are in the poppy genus. The Opium Poppy and all the other poppies that produce opium-like substances are in this genus.

The poppy family's sub-families and genera are listed below. The number of species in each sub-family is given in parentheses.

The Poppy Family

I. Chelidonioideae Subfamily (20-30 species)

    A. *Tree Celandines* (Bocconia)

    B. *Greater Celandine* (Chelidonium)

    C. *Eastern Horned Poppies* (Dicranostigma)

    D. *Snow Poppy* (Eomecon)

    E. *Horned Poppy* (Glaucium)

    F. *Forest Poppy* (Hylomecon)

    G. *Plumed Poppies* (Macleaya)

    H. *Bloodroot* (Sanguinaria)

    I. *Celandine Poppies* (Stlophorum)

II. Eschscholzioideae Subfamily (17 species)

A. *Tree Poppies (Dendromecon)*

B. *Californian Poppies (Eschscholzia)*

C. *Tulip Poppy (Hunnemannia)*

III. Papaveroideae Subfamily (150+ species)

A. *Desert Poppies (Arctomecon)*

B. *Prickly Poppies (Argemone)*

C. *Pygmy Poppies (Canbya)*

D. *Woodland Poppy (Cathcartia)*

E. *Blue Poppies (Meconopsis)*

F. *True Poppies (Papaver)*

G. *Long-fruited Poppies (Roemeria)*

H. *Californian Tree Poppies (Romneya)*

I. *Wind Poppy (Stylomecon)*

IV. Platystemonoideae Subfamily (15 species)

A. *Meconellas (Meconella)*

B. *Cream Cups (Platystemon*

C. *Platystigmas (Platystigma)*

The Poppy Name

THERE ARE MILLIONS of known plant and animal species. Biologists have a difficult job keeping track of all of them. So they use a naming system for organisms to eliminate any ambiguity and confusion.

Common names usually define a plant by the way that we think about plants—family, broad, and species, specific. So the common name "Opium Poppy" refers to the fact that it is the opium species of the poppy family—and that's all. For botanists, this creates problems. To start, they would need to come up with hundreds of different adjectives to describe each species of poppy. This would almost certainly lead to longer names, such as "Poppy that is Red with Four Petals and No Leaves." More important, the names of all the poppies would say nothing about how any two poppies were related.

Archaic System

SUCH PROBLEMS ARE NO BIG DEAL to most of us. A person who can name five different poppies is unusual. But to the scientists who study hundreds of different poppies, these problems are unacceptable. As a result, they have adopted a naming system to fix these problems. Developed by a Swedish botanist named Carl von Linne, this system is familiar to most people, even if it still seems strange and archaic. It is familiar because the scientific names of things are often mentioned in newspaper articles and museum literature; it is strange and archaic because it uses Latin for the names, a language few of us know.

Simple System

EACH PLANT IS GIVEN two Latin names. The first is the genus of the plant, given in the form of a noun and capitalized. A genus is a group of related species. For example, all true poppies are of the genus *Papavera*. The second name used to describe a plant is the species, and it identifies the specific member of the genus. This name is not capitalized and it is normally an adjective. The Opium Poppy is thus named *Papavera somniferum*.

The Linne system for naming plants works exactly as does everyday speech, although the use of Latin names makes it a little more confusing. The poppy used almost exclusively for opium production is commonly referred to as the Opium Poppy. This is the name of the kind of flower, poppy, with a descriptive word to clarify what kind of poppy—opium. The scientific name for this flower is *Papavera somniferum*. The first word, *Papavera*, or poppy, is the genus of the flower. The second word describes the kind of poppy it is: *somniferum*. This is two Latin words combined: *somnus*, meaning "sleep," and *ferre*, meaning "bring." So the Latin phrase for the opium poppy means, sleep bringing poppy.

Regardless of what language a botanist speaks, he will always refer to the opium poppy as *Papavera somniferum*. When reading non-scientific literature, the opium poppy will be referred to in an almost limitless numbers of ways. Below is a list of names for the opium poppy in a number of languages. In addition to showing how some languages are similar to others, it shows how important the opium poppy is to cultures throughout the world.

Poppies Around the World

Language	Poppy Name
Bengali	Afing-gach, Posto
Burmese	Bhainzi
Dutch	Papaver
English	Opium Poppy
French	Pavot Somnifère
German	Mohnblume
Gujrati	Khas-khas
Hindi	Post, Khas-khas, Post Dana
Hungarian	Mák, Kerti Mák
Italian	Papavero
Japanese	Hinageshi
Laotian	Za Zang
Malayalam	Kashakasha
Polish	Mak Lekarski
Portuguese	Papoula
Punjabi	Post
Romanian	Mac
Sanskrit	Ahiphena
Spanish	Adormidera, Amapola
Swedish	Vallmo
Tamil	Postaka
Thai	Ton Fin
Turkish	Hashhash Tohumu
Urdu	Khas-khas

14
Horticulture

THE MOST USED CONSTITUENT OF OPIUM is morphine and so poppies that produce the highest amount of morphine are those that are cultivated. Today, only one poppy is used to any extent for the production of opium, *Papaver somniferum,* although this was not always the case.

There are a handful of poppy varieties that produce opium-like substances. *Papaver rhoeas* contains many of the same alkaloids found in opium, including non-trivial, but still small, amounts of morphine. *Papaver rhoeas* is known as the Common Poppy and Flander's Poppy, as well as Corn Poppy. In Europe, the flower is a symbol of the dead from the two world wars. Recall that the Oriental Poppy—*Papaver bracteatum* and *Papaver orientale*—produces trivial amounts of morphine, but large thebaine concentrations. While the rest of the poppy genus generally do not produce substances with a great similarity to opium, all produce interesting alkaloids.

Opium Poppy

THERE IS ONLY ONE SPECIES of poppy that produces high morphine yields—*Papaver somniferum.* Another poppy, *Papaver setigerum,* has a lower, but still high morphine yield. It is not a species itself, but a subspecies of *Papaver somniferum. Papaver setigerum,* on the other hand, is quite different from the dominate somniferum varieties, being one-third the size. Many believe that setigerum is the direct, wild descendant of the larger somniferum of today. It is likely that this smaller plant has been cultivated and human-selected to produce more opium.

Papaver somniferum has a number of varieties. All have large, golf-ball sized, slightly oval-shaped seedpods. It is when the plant blooms that the different varieties become clear. The most striking of these differences is the flower color.

Flower Color

ALL OF THE FLOWER PETALS of opium poppies are large, two to five inches across, and brightly colored. The "classic" opium poppy color is a rich red, but poppies are also found in

Poppies come in differing hues of red and blue.

differing hues of red and blue. The red flowers often take the form of pink and the blue flowers are more commonly purple, with some being so dark they are almost black. Poppies are also found with stark white petals, perhaps a long-term evolution from a subspecies of yellow poppies that no longer exists.

Horticultural Properties

IN ADDITION TO THE DIFFERENCES in petal color, each variety has slightly different horticultural properties and morphine yields. Farmers plant different varieties depending on their region, weather, and experience. Some varieties are more insect resistant, some more drought resistant, while others may grow better with less sun, more sun, cooler temperatures, or in a slightly different soil type. In the end, however, seed availability is a critical factor, because a farmer cannot plant seeds he does not have. Over time, he will select out the best variety for his location. This is undoubtedly the reason for the large number of Opium Poppy subspecies.

Opium Yields

ALTHOUGH POPPIES ARE COMMONLY GROWN for their seeds and ornamental qualities, the vast majority are grown to produce opium. More specifically, the poppies are grown to produce morphine and the quality of opium is a measure of its morphine content. Considering these issues, poppy farmers wish to maximize two quantities: the morphine concentration of the opium produced and the amount of opium produced.

Morphine Fraction

USUALLY, OPIUM CONTAINS 10% to 15% morphine. Bad crops can contain substantially less morphine, and some contain more. The former USSR state Kirgizistan, which is near Afghanistan, is said to produce some of the highest morphine-yield poppies in existence, with their opium containing roughly 17% morphine.

There are three types of commercial opium production: licit traditional, licit straw, and illicit. *Licit* production is for the legal market which uses the traditional harvesting method of scoring the poppy pods and scraping off the opium that oozes out onto the pod. *Licit straw* is a new manner of harvesting that takes the whole plant, or straw, grinds it up, and extracts the alkaloids. Illicit production is always done in the traditional manner for the illicit markets, mostly heroin.

Amount Produced

ALTHOUGH MORPHINE CONTENT can vary substantially, the amount of opium produced per unit area of land is even more variable. Data on this comes from the United Nations. The table below shows that even the global averages for the three types of cultivation deviate by 300%. Area is given in hectares and yield is given in kg of opium per hectare planted. The unit kg/ha is pretty much the same as pounds per acre. A kg/ha is about 90% a lb/acre.

Types of Cultivation

Cultivation Type	Area	Yield
Licit Traditional	12,000 hectares	31kg/ha
Licit Non-Traditional	24,000	10k
Illicit Traditional	250,000	15k

The differences from country to country—not to mention field to field—can be even greater as seen above. As one example, in 19th Century United States, production as high as 140 kg/ha were reported.

Traditional Cultivation

Country	Area	Yield
India	12,000 hectares	29kg/ha
China	240	83
Japan	1	7

Cultivation

PAPAVER SOMNIFERUM IS RELATIVELY EASY to cultivate under the right range of conditions. There are four resources that must be controlled for optimal growth: soil, light, heat, and water.

Each of these resources affects the final outcome for the plant and its products.

Soil

THERE IS A DEBATE over the type of soil the opium poppy prefers. Some say it prefers a limey soil. Others say the poppy prefers a rich black soil. Rich black soils indicate a high nitrogen content with a neutral pH. This kind of soil is good for growing any kind of plant. It is likely that poppies grow best when they have nitrogen-rich soil with a high lime content. The soil in the central poppy-growing areas of Northern Thailand is rich and black, and surrounded by limestone cliffs, indicating that the soil is likely rich in both nitrogen and calcium carbonate, or lime.

Nitrogen

LIME IN SOIL GIVES it a slightly alkaline pH. Some sources say that poppies grow best in a slightly acidic soil. Conflicting information that poppies grow best in alkaline, neutral, and acidic soils is probably due to differences in poppy variety and the fact that they all grow well under any reasonable conditions. For optimal opium production, however, the most important element in the soil is nitrogen. It is the most vital nutrient for healthy plant growth. It is like blood in an animal body, facilitating the transport of cellular-level nourishment to the plant.

> *Nitrogen is like blood in an animal body.*

Minerals

MINERALS ARE IMPORTANT to the proper functioning of any organism, where they typically help to perform specific functions. Calcium, for example, maintains the acid-base balance of animals, and is necessary for the contraction of smooth and skeletal muscles for movement. Sodium helps animals retain water and avoid dehydration. Both of these minerals are critically important to the poppy, but for very different reasons. Calcium accelerates plant growth and, most importantly, encourages the formation of the alkaloids that make up opium. Sodium, in addition to being used by the poppy to accumulate alkaloids, helps to store those alkaloids once they are created. Other minerals, such as phosphorus and magnesium, while very important for animal health, have little effect on poppy growth and alkaloid production.

Light

LIKE ALL PLANTS, light is necessary to poppies because it is their source of energy. Too much light, however, has a negative effect on the quality of opium produced by the poppy.

> **High contrast between the daytime and nighttime temperatures promotes high morphine yield.**

Morphine Production

MORPHINE IS THE FIRST ALKALOID to mature and reach its maximum level in the poppy. When this level is reached, morphine production more or less stops. Poppy variety, temperature, and light determine the maximum morphine level. Since the maximum morphine content is reached early on in the poppy's development, sunlight is good in the early stages, but needs to be limited later on.

Methylization

AS WE'VE SEEN, MORPHINE IS ALMOST IDENTICAL to two other important opium alkaloids: codeine and thebaine. Codeine is morphine with a single methyl group tacked onto it. Thebaine is morphine with two methyl groups tacked on. Morphine is converted into codeine and thebaine through a process known as methylization. The more sunlight a poppy absorbs, the more methylization it goes through. As a result, sunny conditions tend to produce opium with smaller yields of morphine and larger yields of codeine and thebaine, whereas cool air temperature and poor light intensity are optimal conditions for maximizing morphine yields in opium.

Heat

THE PRODUCTIVITY OF A PLANT begins with the germination process. Temperature variation and distribution are particularly important during this stage. Germination generally occurs between 8°C and 35°C. The plant, however, likes a fairly high variation between the day and night temperatures.

Morphine Yield

FOR MAXIMUM OPIUM YIELD with a high morphine content, it is best to have a high contrast between the daytime and nighttime temperatures. This is true for all the stages of plant development, but it is of paramount importance in the germination and maturity stages. As the plant progresses from germination through the various stages of capsule formation, the mean optimal temperature rises. At germination, the optimal temperature is 13°C, increasing to 22°C at maturity.

Seed Yield

POPPY SEEDS ARE WIDELY USED in cooking. An optimal temperature for producing opium is not the same as for producing seeds. A temperature that is lower during the growing season than is optimal for opium production produces a larger, heavier capsule filled with more seeds. Seed yield can vary up to 50% depending on the temperature.

Water

THE ROOTS OF THE POPPY PLANT are very sensitive to rot. At the same time, the plant requires a fairly large supply of water. Optimally, poppies want a soil that is roughly half saturated with water—slightly more or less depending on the stage of development. As a result of this, poppies must be planted in a well-drained soil. Poppies are often cultivated on hillsides with slopes of 20° to 40°. This serves two purposes: it keeps the soil well drained and provides a large diurnal temperature variation.

15

Agriculture

TWO KINDS OF OPIUM AGRICULTURE are prac-
ticed—traditional or *seed pod scoring*, and non-
traditional or *straw extraction*. The differences
in the methods involve how the plant is
harvested, which has a profound effect on the opium
produced. The straw method is notably inferior to
the scoring method.

Planting

POPPY SEEDS ARE SMALL AND SPHERICAL, just like those
on a poppy seed bagel or Kaiser roll. Although most
poppy seeds are black, they are also found red and
blue; before maturation, they are white. Poppy seeds
are not germinated before they are planted, as is the
practice with many plants. This is because they are so
delicate, the germination would destroy them. Instead,
they are simply mixed with soil and scattered about
the ground. The ground is then watered. The farmer
must be careful not to over-water the seedlings because of the poppy vulnerability to root rot. Also,
they must be protected from air and water currents
so they won't be transported far away.

Thinning

WHEN THE SEEDLINGS ARE ROUGHLY a half-foot tall, the poppy field is thinned. In areas where the plant density is too high, plants are transplanted. By this time in the plant's development, it is strong enough to be moved. Care is taken to ensure the plants root well and maximize their intake of nutrients from the soil, instead of competing with other plants. To maximize the opium yield, the plot must be weeded to remove invading plants as well as poorly developing poppies.

Harvesting

THE PLANTS TAKE ABOUT FOUR MONTHS to mature from germination to harvest. The opium is harvested when the plants have bloomed and the leaves have fallen off. The opium is extracted from the poppy's seedpod, or "bulb," which ranges in size from a golf ball to a tennis ball. It is round and smooth. Its color is initially in the range from pale green to gray. The two kinds of opium agriculture are distinguished by how the opium alkaloids are extracted from the seedpod.

Seed Pod Scoring

ABOUT TWO WEEKS after the leaves have fallen off the poppy, the pods are ready to be scored, meaning they are cut with shallow lines. The exact time for the harvesting occurs when the area of the pod where the flower petals had attached turns dark.

Some opium farmers say the pods should be slashed vertically—others horizontally. Another common procedure combines the two so that the pod is slashed in the shape of a saw-tooth. Any slashing geometry will work. Slashing horizontally is more complicated, because the cuts must be dashed. Vertical slashes may be made in long cuts from the top of the pod to the bottom.

Scoring Depth

THE SEEDPOD HAS TWO CHAMBERS. The distance between the inner and outer walls is small, a maximum of

━━━━━━━

Depth of the cuts depends upon the size of the pod.

perhaps a quarter inch. The inner chamber holds most of the poppy seeds. The outer chamber contains the latex that will become opium. If the cut into the seedpod is too deep, the inner wall will be cut and the latex will flow into the seed chamber and be lost. As a result, care must be taken to cut the seed pods deep enough to get through the outer wall, but not so deep as to cut through the inner wall. In the book, *Opium Poppy Garden*, William Griffith provides maximum cut depths for poppy seedpods of different sizes. For small seed heads, with diameters of up to three-quarters of an inch, he recommends a maximum depth of only one-sixty-fourth inch, requiring quite a steady hand!

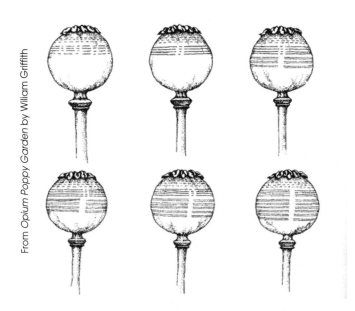

From *Opium Poppy Garden* by William Griffith

Successive Cuts for Milking Seedpod

Frequency

MUCH HAS BEEN WRITTEN about at what times of the day the poppy seedpods should be scored and the opium scraped. It appears that this does not matter too much, except that if the opium is allowed to dry too thoroughly on the seed pod, it can flake off and be lost. Therefore, it is best to scrape the pods in the morning before the hot sun has a chance to dry the opium. This means the pods should be scored the evening before.

The harvesting process is repeated each day.

On poppy farms, the harvesting process is repeated each day. At dusk, farmers go into the poppy fields and score the poppy pods. The next morning, before the sun is even up, the farmers come back out to the fields to scrap off the now red-brown substance that has formed on the outside of the seedpods. During a good year, the plants are scored every two to three days, up to five times for each plant during its lifetime.

Straw Harvesting

IN THIS FORM OF HARVESTING, the seedpod is removed from the plant and ground up. The resulting substance is not opium, but it does have most of the alkaloids found in opium. These alkaloids are then isolated from the straw. This method of cultivation is only used in licit production, and even there it is not the preferred production method because it cannot be used to obtain thebaine and other important, but minor, opium alkaloids.

Poppies do not deplete the soil of nutrients.

16
Tribal Production

OPIUM PRODUCTION IS AN IMPORTANT PART of the economies of many remote tribes throughout the world. The best-studied tribe is the Hill Tribe Indians. They are located deep in the Golden Triangle, the area where Northern Thailand, Burma, and Laos meet. Here, the opium poppy is indigenous and the seeds have been cultivated for over 3000 years.

The study of the Hill Tribe Indians dispels two common myths about the effect of illicit opium production on poor cultures. The first is the idea that opium destroys their cultures by causing rampant opium addiction. In fact, opium addiction is not common and it does not have a large effect on indigenous cultures. The second myth is that opium is grown at the expense of growing food and other staples. Actually opium is produced in addition to their "normal" crops and provides much needed medicine and gold, which can be traded for other needed commodities.

Cash Crop

POPPIES ARE A CASH CROP that has little effect on the agriculture of subsistence farming. The poppies are grown during the dry season when staple crops of rice and corn cannot be cultivated. In addition, the poppies do not deplete the soil of nutrients. They have been known to grow on the same field for 20 consecutive years without the need for a rest or nutrient replenishment. So opium cultivation does not take away from land that could be used to grow food. Except for harvest, poppy cultivation requires less attention than the traditional food crops grown.

The advantages of poppy agriculture for the Hill Tribe Indians is easy to see. Its growth takes place during periods of time when the fields would be fallow, thus it does not interfere with food production. It requires relatively little work while bringing in a cash profit, usually paid by opium merchants in an inflation-proof currency such as gold or silver bars. Equally important, the Hill Tribe Indians are able to stock their herbal pharmacy. They use opium for relief of pain, diarrhea, and coughs. The opium is also used ceremonially by tribal elders.

Little Regulation

THE HILL TRIBE PEOPLE LIVE DEEP in the jungle, where no centralized government has meaningful power. Transportation is limited to donkey, helicopter, and the small airplanes which can land on one of the few air strips. Its remoteness, both in terms of geography and communication, make control of the region an expensive proposition. Given the small number of people who live in the area, it does not make sense for the national governments to waste resources there. The only external power in the region is provided by the drug distributors.

The members of the tribe are often hostile toward the government, because their survival is highly dependent upon their opium cultivation. The Hill Tribe People live dangerously close to starvation. Opium production allows them to have the equivalent of a savings account to use in hard times.

Caught in the Middle

THE BAD ASPECT OF THIS SITUATION is that it puts the Hill Tribe People in between the government and the drug distributors. When the government decides to "crack down" on the drug trade, whole communities are devastated by military raids with heavily armed men in helicopters. The crops are destroyed. Similarly, lower global opium yields brings lower quality opium and heroin to the market. So the little guys—the farmers and people dependent on opium and heroin—get hurt in these clashes between the government and the drug industry. The big players making the large profits remain unscathed.

The story of opium is romantic and enticing.

Despite the problems, opium is an important part of the economic life of the Hill Tribe People and other indigenous groups around the globe. The possibility of the government destroying their crops and thus causing much hardship, including starvation, is of little concern compared to the certainty of starvation without opium agriculture.

Grapes, Not Poppies

THE THAI GOVERNMENT IS HIGHLY COMPLICIT with United States drug policy. They started a campaign to offer the natives alternatives to opium production—in particular, wine production. There are many problems with this idea. While wine production is legal, it is not nearly as profitable as opium. It required upsetting the food agriculture, with questionable profits, taking years to development.

> *Introducing a new drug into a culture is risky.*

There is also some concern about introducing the native population to alcohol. Drug taking is a social activity, and introducing a new drug into a culture can have baneful consequences to that culture. This has been seen when Native Americans were introduced to alcohol, as well as when the Chinese were introduced to opium. The Hill Tribe People have a long history of using opium. Its use is part of their culture and cultural rituals keep it in check. No such rituals exist for alcohol use and could take generations to develop.

17
Distribution

THERE ARE TWO DISTRIBUTION CHANNELS for opium: licit and illicit. Neither is what could be called a "free market." The licit distribution is tightly controlled by governments, even to the extent of requiring government approval of prescriptions for people to buy small amounts for personal use. The illicit distribution of opium is a "freer" market than the licit distribution, because anyone may buy and sell opium at consumer set prices. But government enforcement of drug laws distorts the market by increasing the cost and by imprisoning, and even killing, those involved in illicit trade.

Licit vs. Illicit Opium

ROUGHLY 85% OF ALL OF THE WORLD'S OPIUM is distributed illegally. Based upon records of the licit production and estimates of the illicit production, rough 600 tons of licit opium and 4000 tons of illicit opium were produced annually at the turn of the 20th Century. Although this may seem like a very large quantity, it really isn't when considered on a global scale. This amount of opium would fit inside about 40 train cars. Looked at another way, the world's daily supply of opium could be delivered in a pickup truck. About 100 million people use opium in one of its many forms on a daily basis. So a pick-up truck filled with opium is not much to supply such a large population. Given the smallness of these quantities, it is not surprising why law enforcement agencies have been ineffectual in stopping the flow of illicit opium.

Licit Opium

TWO PRODUCTION PROCESSES ARE USED in the licit trade. The first is the traditional process of scoring the poppies and collecting opium. The second is the new process where the poppy plants are cut and the resulting straw is ground up. The opium alkaloids are then extracted from this ground-up, opium-like substance.

The United States encourages its opium suppliers to use the latter manufacturing process because it is less prone to "leakage," or the routing of licit opium into the more profitable illicit market. There has been much resistance to using this method, however, because extraction of thebaine and other minor alkaloids is difficult.

The table below lists opium-producing countries, their yearly opium production in tons, and the harvesting method they use.

Countries Producing Licit Opium

Country	Yield	Method
India	346 tons	Scoring
Australia	102 tons	Straw
France	63 tons	Straw
Turkey	54 tons	Straw
China	20 tons	Scoring
Spain	14 tons	Straw
Hungary	12 tons	Straw

Processing

THE LOCATIONS WHERE OPIUM is produced and where it is
processed are distinct. India produces 60% of the
world's licit opium, but processes only a little over 10%
of the world's licit opium. In contrast, the United States
produces no licit opium, but processes 60% of that
produced by other countries. Most of this opium, almost
90%, is used to supply the market for codeine and
morphine. The rest goes to create semi-synthetic opioids
like hydrocodone. What is interesting about these numbers is that roughly 50% of all of the morphine found
in opium is converted to codeine, which constitutes
90% of the codeine on the market. This does not make
much sense, because morphine is a safer drug than
codeine and can be used as well or better than codeine
in all therapeutic applications, but at much lower doses.
The reason for converting morphine to codeine is
concern for addiction.

The final products of licit opium worldwide are
listed below. Each drug is given with the percentage it is
of all products, by weight. So, for every 100kg of all the
drugs, there are 45.8kg of morphine produced.

Licit Opium Products

Drug	Proportion
Morphine	45.8%
Codeine	42.5%
Dihydrocodeine	5.4%
Pholcodine	1.9%
Hydrocodone	1.5%
Thebaine	1.4%
Oxycodone	0.9%
Ethylmorphine	0.6%

Illicit Opium

MOST OF THE WORLD'S ILLICIT OPIUM is converted into heroin because it is safer and cheaper to smuggle a small amount of heroin than a large amount of opium. It requires roughly thirty times as much opium as heroin to produce the same effect. So opium is plentiful on the black market primarily in Southeast Asia, and other places which are close to the growing regions.

There are four important opium-producing regions in the world. The most important is Southeast Asia, also known as the "Golden Triangle," It is responsible for roughly 70% of the world's illicit opium. Next is West Asia or the "Golden Crescent", which is responsible for as much as a quarter of all illicit opium. Opium was not widely produced in South America until the mid-1980s. Production there is mostly in Colombia, which accounts for roughly 5% of the world's opium. Mexico is responsible for roughly 1% of the world's opium. Almost all of the opium produced in the Americas goes to produce heroin for the United States market.

Home Grown

OPIUM IS NOT COMMONLY FOUND in the United States. As a result, American opium aficionados ingest one, or many opioids in pill form, or create their own opium, from store bought poppies or by growing it.

Sometimes people sell what they claim is opium on the streets, but it is usually not actually opium. Often, it is black tar heroin, which looks like opium. Another kind of so-called "opium" sold on the streets, called Red Rock Opium, is not even a drug. There is a debate as to what it actually is. Most likely it is a variety of Dragon's Blood Incense.

Most illegal heroin comes from illegally grown poppies.

Even though Red Rock is not a drug, buying it is still illegal. Authorities call it "attempted possession of a controlled substance." In one of the many ironies of the drug laws in the United States, a person selling incense as opium would most likely be subject to a misdemeanor, whereas the person buying a bogus drug and being cheated would be subjected to a felony.

18
Home Grown

OPIUM POPPIES have many uses besides use as drugs. They are used as a source of the poppy seeds that are used widely in cooking. United States federal law mentions poppy seeds as the only part of the plant that is not illegal. The dried plants can be used for various craft projects. And, of course, they are beautiful additions to a flower garden. Noted English botanist Christopher Grey-Wilson—no lover of opium— gushes when talking about this species:

> All these plants are vigorous, sometimes reaching 1.5 m tall so they require plenty of space to develop. They are certainly an arresting sight in full flower...dare one say that some are almost too gaudy for the average garden? ...All of them have a pleasing, though somewhat heady fragrance, much loved by bees.

Grow a Flower, Go to Jail

GROWING OPIUM POPPIES IS ILLEGAL in the United States. However, as long as the plant is not used for opium production, gardeners are usually left alone. Enforcement is usually limited to being told to remove the "dangerous" plants or having drug agents rip out one's garden.

There are many varieties of Opium Poppy that don't much look like the classic Opium Poppy. *Papaver setigerum*, for example, is one-third to one-half as tall as "normal" with a seedpod that is equally deficient. Instead of the brilliantly colored flowers normally associated with this species, setigerum flowers are pale purple.

Other countries have more relaxed laws, or no laws at all, regarding this flower. Foolish is the Opium Poppy gardener who does not know the laws of his location.

Weeds Outlawed

ONE REASON SMALL-SCALE OPIUM POPPY cultivation is accepted in the United States, even though it is technically illegal, is the fact that the plant's growth is so robust. Many writers have likened the Opium Poppy to a weed because it can easily take over a garden. Grey-Wilson admonishes the gardener to "rogue out" poor-colored varieties "the moment they come into flower" lest the garden be taken over by the dreaded pastel poppy. Opium Poppies are found in many gardens as "volunteers," rather than by active cultivation.

Seeds

THE OPIUM POPPY IS ACTIVELY CULTIVATED, which becomes obvious when browsing through a seed catalog. Although the federal drug authorities have been applying constant, gentle, and quiet pressure on seed companies, it is still possible to legally buy Opium Poppy seeds. The implication is that if a person is buying seeds from a seed company, they plan to plant them. Most seed companies limit the number of seeds they will sell to one customer, or have stopped stocking them altogether. The giant United Kingdom seed company Thompson & Morgan no longer ships Opium Poppy seeds to U.S. addresses, for example. They are still available to customers in the United Kingdom, however.

Many super-markets carry poppy seeds.

Seed Companies

BUYING OPIUM POPPY SEEDS from reputable sources has two advantages. First, the seeds are sold to be grown, which means the seeds will be viable and germinate. Second, it is possible to buy specific varieties of Opium Poppies. Neither of these issues is particularly important to the gardener who is attempting to grow the poppies for opium production. Ironically, the government pressure on seed companies hurts those gardeners growing opium poppies for legal reasons.

Covert gardeners have good cause to stay away from seed companies as a source of opium poppy seeds. Certainly, the government will eventually audit the seed company records to determine who has bought *Purchasing* Opium Poppy seeds. Such searches *from seed* have been found to be unconstitu- *companies is* tional in the United States, but this *risky.* will change. In any case, seed-buying history is likely to be admissible in a case against a poppy grower. Any gardener prosecuted for Opium Poppy growing will be in a much worse legal position if the state can prove that he knew that he was growing Opium Poppies.

Supermarket Opium

THE EASIEST WAY TO GET POPPY SEEDS is simply to buy some from a gourmet-cooking store. Such seeds are reported to be sterilized, but the experience of gardeners who have experimented is that most do germinate. Many supermarkets carry poppy seeds. These are likely to be of a lower quality than the "gourmet" variety, but gardeners have reported luck with these as well.

Dried Poppies

ANOTHER OPTION FOR ACQUIRING POPPY SEEDS is to get them from a bouquet of dried poppies. As with seeds from seed companies, dried poppies are becoming harder to find in the United States. But they are still to be had, however, and the seeds found in them are usually viable.

Breaking Two Laws

A FINAL OPTION FOR ACQUIRING SEEDS is to steal them. As already noted, the Opium Poppy is widely cultivated. Many people do not know they are even growing Opium Poppies. It is also possible to steal such plants after they have bloomed, and take the seeds from them. It should be noted, however, that doing so is not just a violation of drug laws, it is property theft.   Getting caught could result in a misdemeanor whereas the accompanying charge, "conspiracy to manufacture drugs," would undoubtedly be a felony.

Cultivation

MOST OF WHAT WE DISCUSSED about commercial poppy production applies to small-scale, personal production. The first decision that must be made is when to plant. This will depend in large part on where the gardener lives. Poppies need a cool temperature to germinate.

Starting

POPPY SEEDS GERMINATE at roughly 60°F, which is 15°C. As a result, poppies are normally planted at the end of fall and the beginning of spring. The plant goes dormant when the temperature gets too cold, and begins growing again when the weather allows. This commonly happens to fall crops grown in areas that have winter snow. If the winter of a particular area is too harsh, the gardener may be limited to one growing season starting in the early spring.

Poppies grow in just about any soil, but they prefer a loamy soil with a high nitrogen content. Gardeners can usually create this kind of soil in their gardens. Because young poppy plants require large quantities of phosphates, gardeners usually add phosphorus fertilizer to the soil before planting.

Planting

PLANTING POPPIES is a little like planting lawn grass. Seeds are sprinkled over the loose soil and allowed to germinate. As with grass, the poppy seeds must be kept moist until they germinate.

Transplanting

THE BIGGEST PROBLEM WITH CASTING SEEDS is that the gardener has little control of where the poppies grow. With many plants, such as marijuana, gardeners germinate the seed outside the soil and then plant a small number of seedlings in an organized fashion. This cannot be done with poppies. The roots of the immature plant are too fragile to germinate outside of the soil. They can, however, be germinated in a pot and then transplanted later. Poppies don't like being transplanted, however, so the best way to is to germinate in peat pots and transplant the whole package, pot included, into the ground.

Poppies are planted late fall–early spring.

Watering

DURING GERMINATION, POPPIES NEED a moist soil. Just the same, their roots are very sensitive to rot and over-watering must be avoided. When the plants are young, they can be killed by the force of a harsh water spay. Careful gardeners use a spay bottle. This is another advantage to germinating in pots because greater care can be given each plant.

Thinning

FOR OPTIMAL OPIUM PRODUCTION, the garden is thinned when the plants reach a height of about a half a foot. The most robust plants are be kept and the rest are removed. The plants are placed in rows and columns with the rows separated by one foot and the columns separated by a third of a foot. Nitrogen fertilizer is added to the soil at this time.

Growing

THE MAIN ISSUES that the grower faces during the growth of the plant are controlling the water and sunlight. Poppies like a lot of sunshine. For the outdoor gardener, there is little that can be done short of praying and relocating. Fortunately, watering can be controlled.

Poppies are more particular about water than they are any other resource. Without a good supply of water, they die. Providing water is usually not difficult. The problem is to avoid saturating the soil. Regardless of the age of the poppy, it is quite prone to root rot. The best way to avoid root rot is to water the soil lightly on a constant schedule. Best is watering twice per day: once in the morning and once in the afternoon. Evening watering should be avoided because it promotes fungus growth.

Flowering

WHEN THE POPPY FLOWERS, its supply of water is dramatically reduced to only as much water as it needs to stay alive. This stress increases the amount and quality of the opium produced by the plant.

Harvest

THE PODS REMAIN on the plant stalks after the flowers drop. Over the next few days, the pods increase in size. After roughly two weeks, the pods are ready to harvest. This is when the gray band where the flower used to be attached become dark.

Milking the Pods

THE SEED-PODS ARE CUT around the top. Each cut is a dashed line with roughly a half-inch cut followed by roughly an eighth of an inch uncut. The depth of the cut depends upon the size of the pod. As time goes on, the pod is cut, further and further down the pod. This process is done daily for up to one month.

If the climate is such that there is no morning dew, the pods can be cut in the evening, and the opium

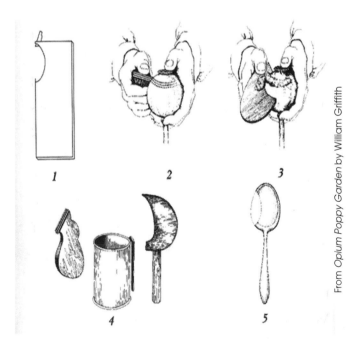

From *Opium Poppy Garden* by William Griffith

Tools used to score seed pods for milking.

harvested the following morning. Otherwise, the cutting is done in the morning and the harvesting in the afternoon. Regardless, in the time between the cutting and the harvesting, the liquid opium dries onto the pods. To harvest, the dried opium is scraped off the pods into a container.

Is it Worth it?

WE KNOW FROM COMMERCIAL OPIUM PRODUCTION that the amount of opium produced on a hectare of land runs anywhere from 10 kg up to 150 kg. The average for commercial licit production is 30 kg. For illicit production, the number is only 15 kg. Based on these numbers, a backyard gardener with a 10-foot by 10-foot plot of poppies would produce roughly 15 grams of opium.

Morphine yield from home grown is small.

Assuming a 15% morphine yield, this would mean the plot would produce 2 grams of morphine or 2/3 gram of heroin. This amounts to roughly $100, which is not a great payoff for the work and brings considerable legal exposure.

Obviously people who grow Opium Poppies on a small scale are not doing it for the drugs they produce, but as a hobby. Perhaps they are interested in the production process for the drug they enjoy. The government's use of resources to stamp out this illegal activity is fatuous. The drug enforcement authorities would have to shut down hundreds of poppy gardens to equal the arrest of one heroin dealer. But this does not stop them. People have been punished with 20 years in jail for growing a small opium garden. Growing an opium garden is a very risky business that should be avoided by all means.

19
Using Opium

WHEN MOST PEOPLE THINK OF OPIUM, they picture men and women lounging in dens smoking it from intricate pipes. However, opium has been more commonly eaten during most periods of history. It is only in the East—especially in China—where opium was commonly smoked.

Eating and Drinking

OPIUM CAN BE EATEN IN MANY FORMS. Harvesters in the poppy fields need simply to lick their fingers and tools to get the effects of opium. This form of opium ingestion has undoubtedly been used for as long as opium itself.

Laudanum

PROBABLY THE MOST FAMOUS FORM OF OPIUM for eating is Laudanum, which is opium dissolved in alcohol and water. This concoction has several advantages. The alcohol preserves the opium if the laudanum is to be stored for a long time. In addition, the alcohol increases the speed with which the opium alkaloids are delivered to the blood stream and decreases alkaloid loss due to removal by the liver.

The down side is that alcohol and morphine to not interact well. At high

Taste of opium improves with experience. enough levels, the two can cause pulmonary edema, in which lungs fill with fluid, causing death. However, this is unlikely due to the low concentrations of both drugs, but a thought to be kept in mind.

There are other Laudanum-like mixtures. Paregoric is basically just Laudanum with camphor. Black Drop is a mixture of opium, water, and ipecac, which is an expectorant and emetic, a vomit-producing drug.

Poppy Tea

OPIUM HAS BEEN INGESTED IN THE FORM OF TEA for a long time. It is not, however, "opium tea," and even saying that one ingests opium in this manner is suspect. The beverage itself is poppy tea, because it is made by steeping ground-up dried poppies. Although it is an effective means of delivering the alkaloids of opium to the body, it is not opium per se that is ingested.

Making Poppy Tea

POPPY TEA IS NORMALLY MADE OUT OF DRIED POPPIES. The seedpods of a couple of poppies are ground up and mixed in a pot with two cups of boiling water, which is immediately removed from the flame. This mixture is stirred and then drained, just like when making any tea.

The resulting tea is not very tasty. It is bitter and has something of a slimy texture that gives one the sensation of sucking on wet weeds. Reactions to the taste run from palat- able to repugnant. Then again, the taste of alcohol is usually considered unap- pealing when it is first tried. As with alcohol, the taste of opium i m - proves with experience, although there are limits. There are various ways to improve the flavor of the tea, such as adding sugar or honey, but none work particularly well.

Adjusting Dose

MOST FIND TWO seedpods per "dose" too conservative a recipe. Ten poppy seedpods is more commonly used with two cups of water. The inexperienced should take care when trying

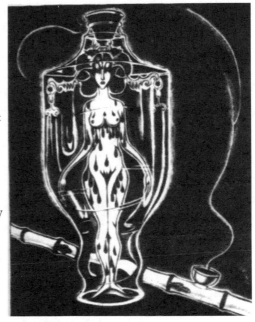

poppy tea, because it takes between ten to thirty minutes to feel the effects. An overdose can happen if one drinks a cup of poppy tea, doesn't feel anything after a few minutes, drinks another, and so on.

Acquiring Poppies

THE POPPIES PEOPLE USE TO MAKE TEA are usually acquired as dried poppies from florists and craft stores. Dried poppies are quite beautiful and are used for a number of decorating purposes. A couple of cups of strong poppy tea could be made from a bouquet of dried poppies.

Although opium poppies are technically illegal in the United States, they are commonly available for purchase legally, but only for legal purposes, like making floral arrangements. Rather than make a big deal out of this disconnect between law and legal commerce, the government has moved quietly and slowly to stop the distribution of opium poppies for craft purposes. They have been more aggressive in stopping illegal uses of poppies, on the other hand. The first man ever prosecuted for possession of opium poppies was acquitted. But that might just be luck of the draw. At least one man is doing twenty years in prison for growing a small patch of poppies. Outside of the United States, most other countries do not control opium poppies on this small scale. It is legal to make poppy tea in many parts of Europe, for example.

Preparation

RAW OPIUM, which is scraped off of the poppy seedpod, contains a number of substances that make it ill-suited for smoking, including water, leaves, twigs, and other plant material. While some users prefer to smoke raw opium, most prefer "smoking" opium. Converting raw opium to smoking opium is easy and can be done in any kitchen.

The raw opium is placed in a vat of boiling water, which causes the alkaloids to dissolve. The plant material does not dissolve. The resulting solution is strained through cheesecloth, which yields a clear brown liquid called "liquid opium." The liquid is heated again over a low flame. The water is slowly evaporated in this way, leaving a dark brown paste. The paste is sun dried until it has a putty-like consistency. The result is smoking opium. When prepared correctly, the yield of smoking opium is equal to roughly 80% of the original raw opium.

Morphine

THE MOST IMPORTANT CHEMICAL PROCESS involving opium is the isolation of morphine. This is just as true for the illicit chemist creating heroin as it is to the licit chemist creating codeine. The process is quite a bit more compli-cated than preparting smoking opium.

The resulting solution—the liquid opium—is heated to a boil. Calcium hydroxide, better known as slaked lime, is added to the boiling solution. The lime combines with the morphine to form calcium morphenate.

The solution is cooled, which causes the other alkaloids to precipitate out. The solution is filtered through a cloth to remove all the particulate matter. The new solution, which is primarily calcium morphenate dissolved in water, is reheated, but not to a boil. Ammonium chloride is added to make the solution slightly alkaline with a pH of 8 to 9.

When the solution is cooled, the morphine precipitates out. The solution is again poured through a cloth filter. The precipitate is sun dried, yielding morphine base, which is a light brown color.

Heroin

WITH A LITTLE MORE WORK, this morphine can be converted into heroin, which is describe in *The Little Book of Heroin*. The morphine must be combined with acetic anhydride—a substance similar to vinegar. The morphine solution is gently cooked with about three times as much acetic anhydride. The result is roughly 70% as much heroin as the original quantity of morphine. Given that heroin is three times as potent a painkiller and euphoriant, this is a very profitable conversion.

Smoking

OPIUM IS RARELY SMOKED. Burning opium the way that cannabis is burned when smoking a joint destroys many of its important alkaloids. When it is smoked, it is combined with another substance such as marijuana or tobacco.

Rather than smoking, opium is vaporized and inhaled. While harder to accomplish, it is safer because few particles are being ingested. In an opium den, the pipes are usually so long that the users can not apply the flame to the pipe bowl. As a result, many people who have used opium in a "den" think they are "smoking," but technically are not doing so. Opium dens are not a thing of the past, they are still big business in places like Thailand.

A third way uses two paper clips, a straw, and a heat source. The straw is held in the mouth. One of the clips is heated lightly so it can melt a small amount of opium that will solidify back onto the clip as it cools. This clip is placed near the end of the straw. The second clip is heated greatly—until it is red-hot. This clip is placed against the opium on the other clip. The heat causes the opium to vaporize. The vapor is then inhaled through the straw. Regular marijuana pipes and "bongs" with metal cookers are also used. The metal is heated and the vapor inhaled through the other end.

Snorting

OPIUM IS RARELY SNORTED—inhaled into the nose where it would be absorbed through the mucus membrane. Doing so requires that the opium be dissolved in water, which is done by gently heating the opium in the water because the alkaloids are not very soluble and the higher the water temperature, the higher the solubility. Once the opium is dissolved, the solution is drawn into an eyedropper or similar device.

The actual snorting takes a fair amount of coordination. The solution must be sprayed out of the eyedropper at the same time the user inhales. If the timing is not correct, the solution drains out of the nose and down the face. To solve this problem, some people use nasal spray bottles instead of eyedroppers, but getting small amounts of solution out of such bottles is difficult.

Rather than smoking, opium is vaporized and inhaled.

Enema

OPIUM ENEMAS ARE ANOTHER METHOD OF USE. Although it requires less dexterity than using the nose, the acidity of the opium can be fairly painful in the sensitive anus.

Injection

OTHER THAN PHARMACEUTICALLY PURIFIED OPIUM like the no longer produced Pantopon®, opium has too much plant material in it to be injected. Even when well filtered, it is dangerous to inject opium and should not be done.

20
Pharmaceuticals

BEFORE THE 20ᵀᴴ CENTURY, most people used opium directly as opium or in a tincture. Today, opium is most often taken as a pill, which contains nothing that is actually found in opium.

Synthetic Opioids

THESE DRUGS ARE USUALLY SYNTHETIC or semi-synthetic. A semi-synthetic opioid is a chemical which is created by chemically changing a natural opioid. Semi-synthetic opioids are usually similar to the natural opioids in structure. For example, heroin—created by mixing morphine with acetic anhydride—has a structure almost identical to morphine.

Full synthetic opioids do not use natural opioids as templates, and so have very little structural similarity to the natural opioids. They also usually have simpler chemical structures. What exactly constitutes a fully synthetic opioid is unclear, however. They are defined as chemicals that produce opioid-like effects. On a more fundamental level, these chemicals act at the opioid receptor sites.

Opioid Pills

OPIOIDS ARE THE DRUG OF CHOICE for the treatment of pain, cough, and diarrhea. Morphine, although it is the king of the opioids, is rarely prescribed for anything but pain for terminal patients—where addiction is a small concern. Codeine is, thus, the only natural opioid widely prescribed. Following are the most common opioids. Although heroin is considered a street drug in the United States and unavailable even with a doctor's prescription, in other countries it is commonly part of the physician's pharmacopoeia.

Diacetylmorphine

DIACETYLMORPHINE ($C_{21}H_{23}NO_5$) is the chemical name of heroin. Heroin is a very simple derivative of morphine and has no psychoactive properties. It, like codeine, is a pro-drug which is dependent upon its chemical transformation to morphine for its effect. Whereas only 10% of codeine becomes morphine, almost all heroin breaks down into morphine. Heroin is more potent than morphine because it can better cross the blood-brain barrier and, thus, get a larger amount of morphine to the brain. It is widely believed, even by doctors, that there is a greater rush associated with heroin than with morphine. This is not the case, although heroin is more soluble than morphine and may be administered by injection at a higher concentration.

Dihydrocodeine

DIHYDROCODEINE ($C_{18}H_{23}NO_3$) is a weak analgesic, similar to codeine in most respects. Like codeine, it is often combined with aspirin and caffeine as an effective headache medicine.

Fentanyl

FENTANYL ($C_{22}H_{28}N_2O$) is an extremely potent semi-synthetic opioid, 100 times stronger than is morphine. Fentanyl is used as an anesthetic and analgesic, particularly as part of surgical procedures. It is sometimes seen on the street—usually as very potent heroin—where it can cause overdose due to its potency.

Hydrocodone

HYDROCODONE ($C_{18}H_{21}NO_3$) is the psychoactive ingredient in the widely prescribed pain-reliever Vicodin®. Its popularity is such that it's now often referred to as "Vitamin V"—the moniker first applied to the popular Valium®. Hydrocodone has the same chemical formula as codeine, but its three-dimensional structure is different. It appears that hydrocodone, like codeine, is a pro-drug, meaning that its pain-relieving ability is due to its chemical transformation into hydromorphine.

Hydromorphone

BETTER KNOWN BY ITS BRAND NAME Dilaudid®, hydromorphone ($C_{17}H_{19}NO_3$) is a semi-synthetic derived from morphine. It is also commonly referred to as "dihydromorphinone." Medically, it is used in the treatment of severe pain and cough and is prized by addicts because it is ten times as powerful as morphine with less tendency to produce nausea. Dilaudid® is available in just about any form imaginable, from cough syrups to ampoules for injection.

Powder Dilaudid® is best known because of the central role it plays in the movie, *Drugstore Cowboy*. The almost religious reverence shown for the substance in the movie is understandable; whereas ampule concentrations max out at 4 mg per ml, powder Dilaudid® can be used to create concentrations that are almost arbitrarily high.

Meperidine

MEPERIDINE ($C_{15}H_{21}NO_2$) is a synthetic opioid, best known as Demerol®. It is primarily used as a substitute for morphine because it produces less muscle spasm, constipation, and cough suppression. It is distributed as a syrup, pill, and injectable solution. Meperidine is rather toxic. At equivalent analgesic doses, it is as much as five times as likely to cause fatal overdose as morphine. It is also the basis of many street derivatives, including the "Parkinson's Disease" producing drugs.

Methadone

METHADONE HYDROCHLORIDE ($C_{21}H_{28}ClNO$) is a fully synthetic opioid, invented in Germany as a substitute for morphine during World War II, when opium distribution was interrupted. It is best known today as a "cure" for heroin addiction. Especially in the United States, it is thought to be better to maintain addicts on methadone than on heroin. Methadone is commonly used to detox heroin-addicted people. It is used medically as a pain reliever.

Methadone

Oxycodone

OXYCODONE ($C_{18}H_{21}NO_4$) is the psychoactive ingredient in Percodan®, mixed with acetaminophen, and Percocet®, mixed with aspirin. In its pure form it is sold as Roxicodone™. It is always administered orally as injection, especially intramuscular and   can cause problems. Oxycodone is a semi-synthetic opioid, manufactured from thebaine, with a chemical structure almost identical to hydrocodone.

Oxycodone

Pholcodine

PHOLCODINE ($C_{23}H_{30}N_2O$) is a weak opioid, used primary as a cough suppressant. It has almost no analgesic properties and is not addictive. In most countries it can be purchased over the counter, but not in the U.S., of course.

Propoxyphene

PROPOXYPHENE ($C_{22}H_{29}NO_2$) is the psychoactive ingredient in Darvon-N® and Darvocet-N®. It is fully synthetic with a strong structural similarity to methadone. Although it is used as a painkiller, it is not particularly effective, being slightly weaker than codeine.

The table lists the popular opioids and their relative strength. "Generic" is the generic name of the drug and "Brand" is the brand name of the drug. When a drug is sold under more than one brand name, the most common brand name is used. "Intra-muscular" (IM) is the number of milligrams of the drug administered intramuscularly to be equivalent to 10 mg of morphine administered intramuscularly. "Oral" is the number of milligrams of the drug administered orally to be equivalent to 10 mg of morphine administered intramuscularly. "Halflife" (HL) is the time, in hours, it takes for half the active form of the drug to be removed from the body.

Other Opioids

THERE ARE MANY OTHER OPIOIDS, each with slightly different effects and potencies. The poppy has been a great stimulant for the development of new drugs for pain, cough, and diarrhea. But opium itself is still used in the treatment of disease in underdeveloped countries.

Strength of Opiods

Opiod		Method		HL
Generic	Brand	IM	Oral	
Codeine	Tylenol® III	130	200	3
Diacetylmorphine	Heroin	5	20	2
Dihydrocodeine	Synalgos®-DC	65	100	3
Fentanyl	Duragesic®	0.1	n/a	2
Hydrocodone	Vicodin®	20	25-30	4
Hydromorphine	Dilaudid®	1.5	7.5	3
Levorphanol	Levo-Dromoran®	2	4	12
Meperidine	Demerol®	60-80	150-250	1.5
Methadone	Dolophine®	10	20	24
Morphine	MS Contin®	10	30/60	2
Oxycodone	Percocet®	10	15-30	3
Oxymorphone	Numorphan®	1	10	1.5
Propoxyphene	Darvon®	n/a	200-300	9

Pantopon

UNTIL RECENTLY, Roche Laboratories manufactured a product called Pantopon®, which was a sterile, injectable preparation of the hydrochlorides of opium alkaloids. In other words, Pantopon® was "opium in a syringe." It was sold as a replacement for morphine. According to Roche, the effect of the drug was essentially that of morphine, but the other alkaloids enhanced the sedative and analgesic effects of morphine at the same time they reduce the undesirable effects, such as nausea.

21
Legal Status

AT THE BEGINNING OF THE 19TH CENTURY, there were no "drug laws" in the United States. The idea that they were needed was new and radical. By the end of the 20th Century, however, people seemed to be are more afraid of drugs than of violent crime. Former United States Customs Service Commissioner William Von Raab illustrated this kind of hysterical fear when he said, "I am concerned about the national debt. I am concerned about international terrorism. But, I'm scared to death about drugs."

Subverting the Constitution

OPIUM AND ITS ALKALOIDS were among the first drugs that the United States government controlled. But it was not an easy thing to do in the early 20th Century. The United States Constitution states clearly that if the government is not explicitly given a power, it does not have that power. Nowhere in the Constitution does it say that the government may control the drugs that people produce, possess, or ingest.

The legal status of a drug does not indicate its dangerousness.

The federal government could not control drug use until the Supreme Court provided a ruling that permitted the government to use its power to tax. In the Marihuana Tax Act of 1937, for example, a penalty of $20,000 fine and 20 years in jail was provided for anyone possessing marijuana without a legal fiscal transfer stamp. Of course, the government didn't issue fiscal transfer stamps. This is why all the federal drug prohibitions before the 1940s are written as tax acts. After the 1940s, any pretense at following the Constitution was abandoned. From then onward, the federal government simply placed legal restrictions on drugs—a clear, and some would say treasonous, violation of the Constitution.

> *Drugs are not illegal so much as are the feelings they cause.*

Federal Drug Schedules

DRUGS WITH A POTENTIAL FOR ABUSE are scheduled by federal law into five categories, which determine the penalties associated with possessing or distributing them. Drugs in Schedule I are illegal to possess even with a doctor's prescription. Drugs in Schedules II, III, IV, and V are legal to possess, but only with a doctor's prescription. The higher the number of the schedule, the smaller is the drug's perceived abuse potential.

Basically, the government arbitrarily decides on a schedule for any drug. Heroin, for example, is a Schedule I drug as opposed to Schedule II. The difference between Schedule I and Schedule II is that drugs in Schedule I have no currently accepted medical use. This is true, only because the government says so. In fact, heroin is commonly used as medicine throughout the world. According to doctors outside the U.S., heroin does have an accepted medical use.

The five schedules of controlled drugs, in the following table, range from I (one) to V (five). "Abuse Potential" (AP) is a measure of how likely a person is to abuse the drug. "Psychological Dependence" (PsyD) is an indication of its pleasurable effects. "Physical Dependence" (PhyD) is an indication of its potential for abuse. In the most extreme case, a person can die without having the drug, such as alcohol. "Medical Usefulness" (Use) indicates whether the drug has an accepted medical use, in the United States. "Safety" (Safe) indicates that the drug is unsafe, even when used under medial supervision. "Example" gives an example of a drug in this schedule.

Schedules

Ssh	AP	PsyD	PhyD	Use	Safe	Example
I	High	Severe	Severe	No	No	heroin
II	High	Severe	Severe	Yes	Yes	morphine
III	Moderate	High	Moderate	Yes	Yes	Vicodin®
IV	Somewhat	Moderate	Low	Yes	Yes	
V	Low	Low	Low	Yes	Yes	Codeine

Scheduling is actually fairly arbitrary. For opioids, it is simple. If a drug is illegal, even with a doctor's prescription, it is Schedule I. If it comes in a form without being mixed with non-opioid drugs, e.g. aspirin, then it is schedule II. Even when mixed with other drugs, if it is a potent opioid, it is Schedule II. Other opioid-containing mixtures, in pill form, are Schedule III. Cough syrups or elixirs are Schedule V. We have not come across an opioid-containing drug that is Schedule IV. Schedule IV seems to be reserved, in large part, for the benzodiazepines, such as Valium® and similar drugs.

Opium and the poppy plant itself are Schedule II. The only exception to this is the seed of the poppy plant, which is not scheduled. This exception exists because poppy seeds are used so widely in cooking. Poppy seeds, however, do contain small amounts of morphine in them, and it is possible to eat enough of them get high. Eating poppy seeds can cause a person to test positive for morphine on a drug test.

There are two reasons why a drug would not be scheduled. First, the drug may not be thought to have an abuse potential, although increasingly the government broadens its definitions of what constitutes "drug abuse" and the list of drugs people are prone to "abusing." But generally, drugs that do not cause psychological changes are not scheduled. The second reason that a drug may not be scheduled is because the government does not know about it.

Analogs

IN THE EARLY 1980s, the government became very concerned about the wave of so-called designer drugs flooding the recreational drug market. That some of these drugs were dangerous, like fentanyl, a heroin-like designer drug that causes Parkinson's Disease, was not the main concern. Because designer drugs were not specifically listed in the law, they were not illegal to manufacture, distribute, and ingest. This was the main concern.

The government cannot schedule a drug that does not exist. Before a drug is scheduled, it is given a Drug Code Number (DCN). Traditionally, this referred to a single chemical. This changed when the Controlled Substances Act was amended in 1986 with The Scheduled Drug Analog Bill, also known as The Designer Drug Enforcement Act. This act defines an analog as any chemical that is substantially similar to a Schedule I or II drug, has stimulant, depressant, or hallucinogenic properties, or is promoted as having these properties in human use. So, in a sense, the drugs are not illegal so much as are the feelings they cause. Since the new law, a drug needn't be specifically scheduled to be illegal. It can simply be similar to a drug that is scheduled.

Sentencing

DRUGS ARE SCHEDULED so that the sentencing of people breaking the drug laws can be standardized. Many drugs, such as heroin and cocaine, are so common that there are sentencing guidelines for the specific drug. Not surprisingly, opium is not included in this list, because it is uncommon in the United States. There are, however, equivalency tables which convert from one drug to another. Thus, 1 gram of opium is equivalent to 0.05 grams of heroin or 0.1 grams of morphine.

Sentencing guidelines for first-time offenders convicted of opium possession are listed in the next table. The sentence depends upon whether the opium is converted to an equivalent amount of heroin, assumed to be morphine and converted to heroin, or assumed to be "Other Schedule I, II, or III Drug." The sentencing is listed in months.

Sentencing Guidelines
First Time Offenders

Amount	Opium	Morphine	Other
<0.10 kg	15-21	37-46	1-7
<0.80 kg	33-41	78-97	8-14
<20.0 kg	121-151	188-235	33-41
<60.0 kg	151-188	188-235	33-41
<200.0 kg	188-235	188-235	33-41

Quantity

THE LAW IS SOMEWHAT MUDDLED on this point, however, because the primary ingredient of opium is morphine. Under the law, a sample of opium can be viewed as impure morphine. In this case, 1 gram of opium would be equivalent to a half a gram of heroin! The reason for this inconsistency is that the government does not take drug quality into account. A person caught with one gram of very pure, 80%, heroin would be treated the same as a person caught with one gram of low purity, 4%, heroin—even though the first person effectively has 20 times as much of the drug.

As a result of this ambiguity, someone convicted of opium possession could be sentenced as though it were opium, morphine, or a unspecified schedule I, II, or III drug. Depending on this choice, the convict with a small amount of opium can get a sentence that ranges from 1 month to almost 4 years.

Mixtures

A DRUG MIXTURE IS DEFINED BY THE DRUG in the mix having the harshest sentence. So if a drug mixture contained 99% codeine and 1% heroin, it is defined as heroin and the amount of heroin would be given by the total weight of the codeine and the heroin.

The many ambiguities in the law make the justice system unpredictable—which defeats the whole purpose. The prosecutor or judge that the convicted person gets determines his sentence, rather than the nature of his crime. These ambiguities also allow those in power to punish certain individuals or groups particularly harshly. Thus, the scheduling guidelines can be used to assure there is no equal justice under the law.

Despite the problems, the sentencing guidelines are helpful. They provide the worst-case scenario to those who are interested in breaking the controlled-substance law. With no criminal record, a person caught in possession of a tiny amount of opium could spend four years in jail.

22

Addiction

WITH ITS FOCUS ON FEAR OF DRUG ADDICTS, the 20th Century could very well be considered "The Addiction Century." In the 19th Century, addiction was simply something that a person liked to do a lot. At that time, addiction was certainly looked on as a vice—the same way we view someone hooked on cigarettes. But Opium addiction was just a vice—it was not the defining characteristic of the person. Many people were addicted to opium in one form or another without even realizing it. Today, addiction is defined more rigorously. The medical definition of an addictive substance requires that it exhibit three qualities: habituation, tolerance, and withdrawal.

Three Essentials of Addiction

Habituation

HABITUATION MEANS that use of the substance is habit forming. This is why something like Drano® could not be considered addictive. It is not something that people find pleasant to ingest and worth doing again, even if they could.

Tolerance

TOLERANCE REFERS TO THE DEGREE to which more of the drug is required on subsequent dosings to recreate the effects experienced when it was first used. Tolerance could be applied to food as well. There is a good discussion in the book, *From Chocolate to Morphine* by Andrew Weil, M.D., about the difficulty in distinguishing drugs from food. Just think of a person in a coma being fed through an IV to get some idea of how confusing it can get.

Withdrawal

WITHDRAWAL IS THE THIRD QUALITY that must be exhibited for a substance to be considered addictive. Withdrawal is experienced when the user abruptly stops using the drug.

Highly Addictive

OPIUM MEETS ALL THREE OF THE STANDARDS and is termed addictive. The fact that a substance is addictive should not damn the drug, however. Caffeine, for example, is an addictive drug and, yet, it is habitually used around the world with little if any damage. Just the same, some drugs thought by many to be quite harmful, such as cocaine, are not technically addictive. Cocaine users do not experience a physical withdrawal syndrome, per se, but a kind of drug "rebound," which is something like a hangover rather than true withdrawal. That some twenty years of research has failed to confirm a withdrawal syndrome shows that the rebound effect is rather small. This does not mean that cocaine is safe. Cocaine is one of the most habit-forming drugs known—far more habit-forming than opium, causing some people to throw away everything of value in their lives for more and more cocaine.

Opium withdrawal can take two weeks.

Dependence

THE WORST THING ABOUT OPIUM ADDICTION is the body's dependency. The body gets violently sick when it does not have a sufficient quantity of the opium upon which it depends. This sickness is called "withdrawal," or the "withdrawal syndrome." It has many symptoms. Many of the alkaloids in opium are addictive, and so the symptoms of withdrawal are a combination of all of the addictive alkaloids.

Withdrawal

MOST OF WHAT IS KNOWN ABOUT OPIUM WITHDRAWAL is based on the morphine withdrawal syndrome, along with anecdotal accounts of actual opium addiction. Most of the withdrawal syndrome of opium is due to the body's physical addiction to morphine, however. A good illustration of this is that morphine alone stops the opium withdrawal syndrome.

To the addict, the most important difference between

opium and morphine withdrawal is that opium withdrawal lasts longer. The worst part of withdrawal from morphine is over in five days. Opium withdrawal is known to stretch out as long as two weeks. Opium withdrawal, however, is less intense than morphine withdrawal.

Drugs that leave the body slowly allow it to "come down" more gradually because the drug is taken away more slowly in a kind of a weaning process. However, as with weaning, the quickly gone intense pain is exchanged for a lingering, not-so-intense pain.

Depression

THE WORST WITHDRAWAL SYMPTOM IS DEPRESSION, because it taints everything else that the sufferer is feeling. Every pain feels much worse. The most important way opium relieves pain is to make us happy. The depression experienced during withdrawal is extreme and tends to trigger a sense of hopelessness. One believes that feelings experienced today are permanent. It is not surprising that withdrawing addicts kill themselves with some regularity; they give up hope.

Addicts feel intense depression because their bodies create too few endorphins and other chemicals needed to feel good. Withdrawing addicts have lower than normal endorphin levels which increase slowly as the body gets back into the habit of creating them.

Insomnia

THE INSOMNIA ASSOCIATED WITH WITHDRAWAL not only exacerbates the depression, it can be hellish all on its own. When sick with a cold or the flu, a person can sleep through much of it. When withdrawing from opium the person is kept awake, which makes the time of withdrawal move very slowly and renders the experience almost unbearable.

Diarrhea and Vomiting

THE DIARRHEA AND VOMITING that accompany withdrawal is often violent. The diarrhea can be almost pure liquid, which is highly acidic, causing the anus to burn. Those withdrawing often experience projectile vomiting, as well. At times they have almost no ability to keep food or liquids down.

Muscle Cramps and "Kicking"

THE MUSCLE CRAMPS that are experienced during withdrawal are the reason for the phrase "kicking dope." The muscles in the legs, usually the location of the worst discomfort, tighten and the sufferer literally kicks in a semi-voluntary manner.

Avoiding Addiction

THERE ARE TWO IMPORTANT QUESTIONS regarding opium addiction. "How long does it take to get addicted?" and "How long does it take to get over addiction?"

Unlike many drugs, like alcohol, it takes very little time of constant opium usage to become addicted. Hospital studies have shown that only three days of daily morphine use causes patients to develop minor physical dependence. Many think that it takes a month to become addicted to opium. While this is not accurate, it does *Limiting use* take at least a couple of weeks for someone *may avoid* to develop a strong dependence that will *addiciton.* result in serious withdrawal symptoms when the drug is no longer taken. Minor addictions do tend to lead to major addictions.

People who wish to use opium without becoming addicted do so by limiting their frequency of use. The rule of thumb is that a person should always refrain from use for twice as long as he used. For example, if he used for two days in a row, he should follow up by not using for four days. Another rule of thumb is that a person should never use more than two days in a row. As the hospital studies have shown, three days will result in a minor addiction. While such withdrawal is not difficult to get through, it is likely the addict will become more addicted given that the cure for his pains is one easy fix away—a fix that will make him feel better even as it is making the addiction worse.

Detoxing

THE LENGTH OF TIME IT TAKES TO DETOXIFY from opium is hard to say. It is common for an addict to get through acute withdrawal, go out and use, and become re-addicted. Just like vacations from work, vacations from pain can make returning to the pain that much harder. Also, it takes roughly a month for the body to get back to producing endorphins properly. Any use in that time upsets the repair the body is doing and lengthens the time until the ex-addict feels good without opium. One to two months is roughly how long it takes for the body to detox and adjust to life without opium.

The process of detoxing an addict from opium is the same as for morphine. The options available include Clonidine, methadone, or other agonist weaning or maintenance, buprenorphine or other agonist-antagonist weaning or maintenance, rapid or antagonist therapy, and "cold turkey"—which is just suffering through the withdrawal without the help of medicine to ease the pain. Even for people who plan to hire someone to detox them, it is best to know and understand the available options.

Cold-turkey is dangerous for those with history of depression or suicide.

It is commonly believed that withdrawal will not kill the addict. While this is mostly true, addicts do die during withdrawal, even if it is not the withdrawal that is directly responsible.

Heat Attack

PEOPLE WITHDRAWING FROM OPIUM experience high blood pressure. For reasonably healthy people with low blood pressure, this isn't a big deal. For an addict who already suffers from high blood pressure, this can be deadly. Such a person should never undergo a cold-turkey withdrawal. They should always have medical supervision for whatever kind of detox they use.

Dehydration

DEHYDRATION IS A DANGER because of all the diarrhea and vomiting that withdrawing addicts experience. It can lead to death if it is not properly dealt with. Anyone going through a cold-turkey withdrawal must take in as much fluid as possible. This can be hard, especially when drinking anything, even water, causes more vomiting. If this is the case, drugs that relieve nausea and vomiting should be administered.

Suicide

PEOPLE WHO KILL THEMSELVES during the course of a detox are probably not looked on with as much sympathy as those who die from dehydration or heart attack. Most people have never experienced the kind of unrelenting, intense pain that opium addicts experience during withdrawal, however. People with a history of suicidal or depressive behavior should stay clear of cold-turkey withdrawal programs and use agonist weaning or maintenance instead.

For more information on opioid detox, see my book *Little Book of Heroin*. Addicts who are considering detoxing themselves should read my book *Heroin User's Handbook*. Both books give a good overview of the process. *Heroin User's Handbook* gives step-by-step instructions.

Bibliography

Grey-Wilson, Christopher. *Poppies*, Timber Press, 1993. Everything you would ever want to know about poppies as flowers. Includes many fine color photographs of the various poppy species.

Griffith, William. *Opium Poppy Garden*, Ronin, 1993. A strange book that tells a story of a young man starting an opium plantation. Mixed in is useful information on growing poppies and the technical aspects of the plant and its cultivation.

Hogshire, Jim. *Opium For the Masses*, Loompanics, 1994. A wonderful overview of opium that is both irreverent and informative.

Kapoor, L.D. *Opium Poppy: Botany, Chemistry, and Pharmacology*, Haworth Press, 1995. This book contains much useful information, but is poorly edited and somewhat tedious.

Latimer, Dean and Jeff Goldberg. *Flowers in the Blood*, Franklin Watts, 1981. Probably the best overview of opium ever written. It discusses all aspects of the drug in a most objective manner.

Lewin, Louis. *Phantastica: Narcotic and Stimulating Drugs, Their Uses and Abuse*, E.P. Dutton & Co., 1964. The original drug classification book—mostly of historically interest.

Moraes, Francis. *Little Book of Heroin*, Ronin, 2000. This book provides a good introduction to heroin.

O. *Opium Poppy Cultivation*, Real Concepts. A nice, short overview of poppy cultivation.

Shulgin, Alexander T. *Controlled Substances*, Ronin, 1992. The standard on United States drug law and particularly useful in converting drug equivalents.

About the Authors

As a physics professor at Portland State University in Oregon, **Francis Moraes, Ph.D.,** became interested in Portland's vibrant heroin subculture. He spent several years studying this subculture in Portland, Seattle, New York, and San Francisco. Dr. Moraes has conducted substantial academic and pharmacological research, and is the author of numerous articles as well as the books *The Little Book of Heroin* and *Heroin User's Handbook.* He is also the managing editor of the hugely popular Internet website www.HeroinHelper.com. He is currently working on a radical self-help manual for the families of drug addicts called "So Your Daughter's a Crack Whore." He is also completing his second novel about an ex-heroin addict whose past makes him a prime suspect when his wife is brutally murdered.

Debra Moraes has a Master's Degree in Acupuncture and Chinese Medicine that she has used to help addicts of opium-derived drugs break free from their dependence. She has spent three years traveling throughout Asia where she has seen first-hand the opium trade and its use and abuse in the cultures there. In recent years she has become increasingly interested in the "methadone maintenance" industry in the United States, and is currently researching the effects of methadone on the entire body.

The Little Book of Heroin

Francis Moraes

ISBN: 0-914171-98-4

$12.95, 96 pg. Illus.

A straight forward look at heroin and who junkies are really. It covers history and the evolution from opium morphine to heroin; how heroin is procured on the "street" and how it is chemically purified; ways heroin is used and diseases junkies get; methods of detox and the real dangers of "sudden death," and much more.

The Little Book of Heroin replaces myths with solid information useful to the user for reducing harm, and to concerned family, friends and professionals who want to better understand.

The word—heroin— calls forth strong emotions, especially fear. It is much like our fear of Satan—an active agent that entices the young and innocent with initial pleasures of the flesh, but once ensnared they face a life of slavery and misery—a living hell.

Such extreme reactions exacerbate the problem. Recreational drug adventures quickly dispel the myth, creating a huge credibility gap. "Everything they said was a lie. I can resist this—if I want to!" Once hooked, or heavily chipping—also called pre-addicted— the victim is no longer innocent and hies in shame, finding refuge with junkie outcasts—instead of seeking help.